Communalism and language
in the politics of Ceylon

NUMBER 2 IN THE PUBLICATION SERIES OF
THE PROGRAM IN COMPARATIVE STUDIES
ON SOUTHERN ASIA

PREVIOUSLY PUBLISHED IN THIS SERIES:

Research on the Bureaucracy of Pakistan
by Ralph Braibanti

ROBERT N. KEARNEY

Communalism and language
in the politics of Ceylon

DUKE UNIVERSITY PRESS

DURHAM, NORTH CAROLINA

1967

© 1967, Duke University Press

L.C.C. card no. 67-28068

Printed in the United States of America
by Seeman Printery, Inc., Durham, N.C.

PREFATORY NOTE

The system of transliteration of Sinhalese words used in this study follows the system for the transliteration of Indian languages contained in A. L. Basham, *The Wonder That Was India* (New York: Grove Press, 1954), Appendix X. The names of political parties and other organizations containing Sinhalese or Tamil words appear in the form in which the organizations themselves cite their names in English, although they sometimes differ from the transliteration of the Sinhalese or Tamil name by the system adopted. It is common, for example, for the dental unaspirated *t* to be rendered as *th* in the forms of these names used in English, and long and short vowels are almost never distinguished.

In Ceylon, the island is frequently referred to in English speeches or writings by its ancient Sinhalese name of Lanka (*Laṅkā* or *Laṅkāva*). Similarly, in recent years it has become increasingly common for "Sinhala" (from the Sinhalese *Siṅhala*) to appear in English rather than "Sinhalese," particularly in references to the Sinhalese language. However, since "Lanka" and "Sinhala" have not as yet become standard English usage outside Ceylon, these terms are not employed in this work, except of course when they appear in quotations, as they very frequently do.

This study is a product of research in Ceylon during 1961-1962 and 1965 and in Great Britain and the United States at various times since 1960. Financial support which made this research possible is gratefully acknowledged from the Ford Foundation Foreign Area Training Fellowship Program, the Joint Committee on Asia of the American Council of Learned Societies and Social Science Research Council, and the Program in Comparative Studies on Southern Asia of Duke University. An expression of sincere gratitude is also due to the many Ceylonese, particularly politicians of all political parties, who gave so generously of their time and talked with almost unexceptionable candor about the problems, issues, and events connected with this study. A scholar could scarcely hope for more ready co-operation, generous assistance, and friendly reception than the author has enjoyed during his stays in Ceylon.

R. N. K.

Santa Barbara, California
September, 1966

CONTENTS

TABLES

MAP

(facing p. 8)

Communalism and language
in the politics of Ceylon

Introduction

Ceylon is endowed with a natural geographical unity, and historical events have produced a political unity. The geographical fact that Ceylon is a small island, only slightly more than 25,000 square miles in extent, has tended to encourage among the peoples who have inhabited it for centuries a sense of identification with the island and of separation from the nearby Indian subcontinent, from which the island's peoples and cultures originated. Although in the 2,500 years of the island's history it frequently contained several separate kingdoms, for 150 years it has been unified politically under a common government. At the time of the first Western intrusion, the arrival of the Portuguese at the beginning of the sixteenth century, Ceylon was divided into three kingdoms. A century later the island's coastal areas had come under European rule, and a single independent kingdom maintained itself in the interior. This condition endured for two centuries through changes from Portuguese to Dutch to British rule of parts of the island. With the demise of the Kandyan Kingdom in 1815, the entire island was for the first time subject to Western political control. After 1833 regional variations in administration were removed and the island was brought under an increasingly uniform and centralized system of administration. The integrity of Ceylon as an administrative unit was reinforced by its separation in 1802 from British India, falling thereafter under the direction of the Colonial Office. Consequently, political developments in Ceylon during the British colonial period followed a separate and often divergent path from those of neighboring India. By the time they attained independence in 1948, the peoples of Ceylon had shared nearly 150 years of relatively centralized and uniform colonial rule as a separate political unit.

The complex of social, economic, political, and ideological changes which have been occurring with particular rapidity since the latter part of the last century have facilitated the integration of the island's population. Roads, railroads, telecommunications, and newspapers spread out across the island and tended to break down regional isolation and bring the population into a single network of transportation and communication. New non-agricultural occupations and social classes cut across the existing social divisions stemming from a feudal, agrarian, traditional society. The city of Colombo became the political, commercial, and intellectual hub of the island. A single centralized administration brought the people under a common governmental system which became of increasing importance with the rapid expansion of the functions of the state. A single government department operated or supervised schools, another built and maintained roads, while a third operated the railroads throughout the island. With the appearance of a participant, competitive political process after the second decade of the present century, the Ceylonese were involved in a common political system and their representatives served in a single legislature. Growing demands for independence emphasized the fact that the inhabitants of the island shared a common political destiny.

Despite the integrative forces of modern times, deep divisions have continued to separate the Ceylonese. Caste, religion, class, and region all have served as focuses of identification and loyalty and have played significant roles in recent Ceylonese politics. Before independence it seemed that caste might become the division of greatest political relevance, but while caste solidarity often is a crucial factor in the locality or constituency, caste questions have not been a source of major political contention. The most important source of division and disruption in Ceylonese politics and the greatest impediment to integrative trends has been the persistence of sentiments of identification and solidarity with broader primordial groups generally referred to as communities.[1]

Community is a term frequently employed in South Asia to denote a people who share a common sense of identity and think of themselves as constituting a unique and separate group, usually on the basis of a distinctive language, religion, social organization, or ancestral origin.

1. A stimulating discussion of primordial group loyalties as an obstacle to the development of a civil state is contained in Clifford Geertz, "The Integrative Revolution: Primordial Sentiments and Civil Politics in the New States," in Clifford Geertz (ed.), *Old Societies and New States* (New York: Free Press of Glencoe, 1963), pp. 105-157. Similarly, see Edward Shils, *Political Development in the New States* ('s Gravenhage: Mouton & Co., 1962), pp. 32-33, and Myron Weiner, "Political Integration and Political Development," *Annals of the American Academy of Political and Social Science*, CCCLVIII (March, 1965), 53-57. As used in this work, the term "integration" refers to what Weiner calls "national integration."

The related term "communalism" refers to an attitude which empha-
sizes the primacy and exclusiveness of the communal group and demands the solidarity of members of the community in political and
social action. In India, community and communalism have most frequently been used in connection with groups delimited on the basis of
religion, particularly the Muslims and Hindus, but have also been employed regarding a variety of social aggregates.[2] Community is at times
used in Ceylon as a euphemism for caste, but usually the term is employed to designate one of the ethnic groups into which the island's
population is divisible—the Sinhalese, Ceylon Tamils, Indian Tamils,
and others.[3] It is in the more frequent sense of the ethnic group that
the term will be used in this study.

   Until recent decades, it was common to refer to ethnic communities
as races and this terminology continues to appear occasionally. The term
"race" has been used in Ceylon census reports since 1911, when it was
substituted for the previously employed term "nationality." The line
dividing a "community" from a "nation" is seldom clear and the larger
communities of South Asia are sometimes called and often claim to be
nations. The Muslims of India prior to independence and partition were
usually considered to be a community, but the contention that they constituted a nation separate from the Hindus resulted in a successful claim
for their right of national self-determination. In Ceylon, both Sinhalese and Tamils argue that their groups possess the tangible and intan-

   2. The term community, it has been noted, is employed in India to describe a
heterogeneous assortment of social units, including religious, ethnic, racial, linguistic,
and caste groups. The common characteristic of communal organizations is the exclusive concern of each with the interests of a particular segment of society. See Richard
D. Lambert, "Hindu Communal Groups in Indian Politics," in Richard L. Park and
Irene Tinker (eds.), Leadership and Political Institutions in India (Princeton: Princeton University Press, 1959), p. 211. Reflecting the complexity of social cleavages in
India, another study has distinguished among "regionalism" based on linguistic and
cultural bonds, "communalism" based on religion, and "casteism." Baldev Raj Nayar,
Minority Politics in the Punjab (Princeton: Princeton University Press, 1966), pp. 5-8.
Also, see Wilfred Cantwell Smith's "An Introductory Essay on Communalism," Modern
Islam in India (Lahore: Sh. Muhammad Ashraf, 1963), pp. 173-216.
   3. There is evidently little serious disagreement on the number of separate communities, their designations, or their composition. Some resentment exists of the name
"Indian Tamil" for the community composed not only of Indian immigrants but of the
descendants of Indians who migrated to Ceylon as long as a century ago. In popular
usage, the Muslims are sometimes referred to as a community although they include
members of three distinguishable ethnic groups, two of which, however, are very small.
The designations used in this study are those employed in the census reports, inappro-
priately labeled the "races" of Ceylon.

gible attributes of nationhood, including a distinctive language, culture, historical experience, ancestral homeland, and a sense of shared membership in the group. The term community, however, encompasses not only the relatively numerous groups with a plausible claim to nationhood, but the much smaller groups which on the basis of some shared characteristic or common origin believe themselves to constitute a group apart.

The community frequently is the most inclusive group possessing a claim on the loyalty of the individual and with which he can readily identify. An individual is born into a community, and membership in that community and exclusion from all others remains with him throughout his life. The community is with rare exceptions endogamous, and intimate contacts tend to be exclusively within it, although impersonal contacts outside the community, such as transactions with traders or government servants, may be a common feature of everyday life. Although relatively little intermarriage occurs, at least in modern times, the significant distinctions are cultural and psychological rather than physical.

Virtually every permanent inhabitant of Ceylon identifies himself and is identified by others as belonging to one and only one community. Although language and religion have played a major role in the development of group self-consciousness and self-identification, even in the few exceptional cases of language or religious ambiguity, identification with a particular community is sharp and clear. In his famous report on the Ceylon census of 1911, E. B. Denham observed of the Sinhalese and Tamils:

In spite of the closest political connection, the two races [i.e., communities] are as distinct to-day in Ceylon as the limits of their settlements are clearly defined. Though Tamils described themselves in the Census schedule as Buddhists, and Sinhalese entered Tamil as the only language they could read and write, it is inconceivable that any Sinhalese would enter himself as a Tamil, or a Tamil as Sinhalese.[4]

The Sinhalese are the majority community of Ceylon, constituting about 70 per cent of the total population (see Table 1). The Sinhalese live in heavy concentrations on the coastal plains of the South and West of the island and more sparsely populate the interior highlands and the

4. E. B. Denham, *Ceylon at the Census of 1911* (Colombo: Government Printer, 1912), p. 196.

Table 1. *Communal composition of Ceylon population, 1953*

Community	Number[a]	Percentage of population
Sinhalese		
Low-Country	3,469,512	42.8
Kandyan	2,147,193	26.5
Total	5,616,705	69.4
Ceylon Tamils	884,703	10.9
Indian Tamils	974,098	12.0
Ceylon Moors	463,963	5.7
Indian Moors	47,462	0.6
Burghers, Eurasians	45,950	0.6
Malays	25,464	0.3
Others	39,550	0.5
	8,097,895	100.0

[a]The preliminary results of a census in 1963 indicated that the total population of Ceylon had climbed to 10,624,507. Although the 1963 census report has not yet been published, it is unlikely to reveal a significant change in the relative size of communities.
Source: Ceylon, Department of Census and Statistics, *Ceylon Year Book, 1962* (Colombo: Government Press, 1963), p. 33.

"dry zone" between the highlands and the northern portion of the island. They were a majority of the population in seven of the island's nine provinces and fourteen of twenty administrative districts at the time of the 1953 census (see Table 2). Outside of the Northern and Eastern Provinces the Sinhalese failed to form the majority in only a single district.

A strong sense of group identity and distinctiveness from neighboring peoples has characterized the Sinhalese for many centuries. A myth of North Indian origin, the possession of a separate language belonging to the Aryan family of languages, and a close attachment to Buddhism have clearly established the separate identity of the Sinhalese from nearby Dravidian-speaking South Indian Hindus. The myth of origin of the Sinhalese, preserved for some fifteen centuries in the ancient Pali chronicle, the *Mahāvamsa*,[5] traces their history from the landing of the North Indian prince Vijaya in Ceylon about 2,500 years ago. Although the assimilation of Dravidian-speaking people into Sinhalese society apparently occurred on a considerable scale over many centuries, the Sinhalese have retained a belief in their descent from North Indian

5. *The Mahāvamsa or the Great Chronicle of Ceylon*, trans. Wilhelm Geiger (London: Oxford University Press, 1912), pp. 51-61.

Table 2. *Major communities by districts, 1953*

District	Percentage				
	Sinhalese	Ceylon Tamils	Indian Tamils	Ceylon Moors	Others
Western Province					
Colombo	80.5	5.3	4.2	4.6	5.4
Kalutara	86.4	1.1	6.6	5.4	0.5
Southern Province					
Galle	94.1	0.6	2.1	2.9	0.3
Matara	94.0	0.6	2.8	2.4	0.3
Hambantota	96.7	0.6	0.1	1.7	0.9
Sabaragamuwa Province					
Ratnapura	75.6	1.6	20.7	1.2	0.9
Kegalla	82.0	1.1	12.4	3.8	0.7
Uva Province					
Badulla	57.1	2.9	35.6	2.9	1.5
Central Province					
Kandy	58.0	3.0	30.5	6.7	1.8
Matale	69.1	3.9	20.2	5.5	1.3
Nuwara Eliya	35.8	2.2	59.2	1.4	1.4
North-Western Province					
Kurunegala	91.9	1.6	1.6	4.1	0.8
Puttalam	53.7	13.5	1.8	29.0	2.0
Chilaw	86.9	5.1	3.6	3.0	1.4
North-Central Province					
Anuradhapura	83.3	6.0	1.5	8.1	1.1
Northern Province					
Jaffna	1.2	95.5	1.6	1.3	0.4
Mannar	4.8	46.3	18.3	24.9	5.7
Vavuniya	16.9	67.1	6.7	8.1	1.2
Eastern Province					
Batticaloa	11.5	47.5	0.7	39.2	1.1
Trincomalee	18.2	40.6	4.1	33.1	4.0

Source: Adapted from Ceylon, Department of Census and Statistics, *Census of Ceylon, 1953*, I (Colombo: Government Press, 1957), 182-183, Table 17.

Aryan-speaking ancestors. The Sinhalese language, spoken only in Ceylon by the Sinhalese, has been a major factor in creating and maintaining the Sinhalese view of themselves as a unique people. Based on Sanskrit and akin to other North Indian Prakrits of the period, the language was brought to the island by the early Aryan settlers. Despite isolation from other Aryan language groups by a wide belt of vastly more numerous Dravidian-speaking people with whom they were in frequent contact, the Sinhalese have preserved their language for more than two

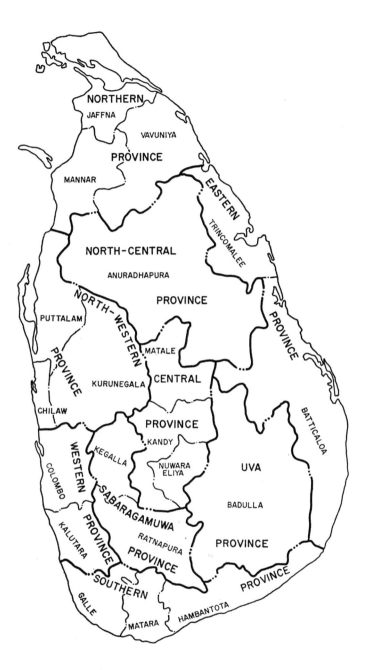

Provinces and administrative districts of Ceylon existing in 1953

millennia. The Sinhalese people and the Buddhist religion are linked by a close and venerable association. Buddhism was introduced into Ceylon in the third century, B.C., according to Sinhalese tradition by Mahinda, son of the great Buddhist Emperor Asoka, and swiftly encompassed the entire Sinhalese people. After the decline of Buddhism in India, the Sinhalese adherence to Buddhism emphasized their distinctiveness from the non-Sinhalese Hindus with whom they had contacts in Ceylon and South India.[6] Despite some conversions to Christianity in the colonial period, the Sinhalese have remained overwhelmingly Buddhist (see Table 3).

Table 3. *Religious distribution of major communities, 1946*

| Community | Percentage | | | |
	Buddhist	Hindu	Muslim	Christian
Sinhalese	91.9	0.1	0.1	7.9
Ceylon Tamils	2.6	80.6	0.2	16.5
Indian Tamils	2.3	89.3	0.3	8.1
Ceylon Moors	0.7	0.3	98.7	0.3

Source: Adapted from Ceylon, Department of Census and Statistics, *Census of Ceylon, 1946*, IV (Colombo: Government Press, 1952), 275, Table 16.

The Sinhalese community in the period of European impact tended toward differentiation into Low-Country and Kandyan Sinhalese, a division that was regional in origin. The Low-Country Sinhalese of the southern and western coastal areas, more than three-fifths of the Sinhalese community, in the course of four centuries of Western influence tended to diverge somewhat in social practices and attitudes from the more traditional Kandyans of the interior, who remained independent until 1815 and were subject to much later and less intense Western and modern influences.[7] The differences between branches of the community

6. On the connection between the Sinhalese and Buddhism and the role of Buddhism in creating Sinhalese group self-awareness, see E. F. C. Ludowyk, *The Footprint of the Buddha* (London: George Allen & Unwin, 1958); and Walpola Rahula, *History of Buddhism in Ceylon: The Anuradhapura Period* (Colombo: M. D. Gunasena & Co., Ltd., 1956).

7. Writing early in the nineteenth century on the differences between Low-Country and Kandyan Sinhalese, John Davy argued that in contrast to the low country, which had undergone considerable change as a result of sustained Western influences, the Kandyan interior probably had not changed in three hundred years. John Davy, *An Account of the Interior of Ceylon* (London: Longman, Hurst, Rees, Orme, and Brown, 1821), pp. 108-109.

did not produce major distinctions of language or culture and failed to create the sense of exclusiveness and distinctiveness which marks off one community from another. With the late nineteenth and twentieth centuries have come rapid advances in transportation and communications. Greater mobility brought many Low-Country Sinhalese to the Kandyan areas as traders, craftsmen, government servants, and planters, and, to a lesser extent, Kandyans moved to the low country in search of employment or education. As a consequence, the differentiation between Low-Country and Kandyan Sinhalese seems to have been declining rapidly. The two branches of the community are not endogamous, except as certain castes are found only in the Kandyan or low-country areas, and with greater mobility and widening horizons marriages between Kandyan and Low-Country Sinhalese have not been uncommon. A lingering sense of separate identification remains and occasionally manifests itself forcefully in politics, generally in the form of Kandyan protests against the severely limited educational and economic opportunities and mounting landlessness in the Kandyan areas.[8] The Kandyan grievances, however, are more frequently expressed in regional than in communal terms, and the political opposition of Low-Country and Kandyan Sinhalese has seldom approached the emotional intensity of the rivalry between communities of recent years.

The principal minority with a claim to long residence on the island is the Tamil community, commonly referred to as the Ceylon Tamils to distinguish them from the much more recently arrived Tamil-speaking people called Indian Tamils.[9] The Tamils, about 11 per cent of the island's population, came to Ceylon from South India in innumerable separate migrations spanning many centuries. They speak the Tamil language, the oldest and most prominent Dravidian language of South India, and are predominantly Saivite Hindus. The Tamils live in the Northern Province, with their heaviest concentration of population on the Jaffna Peninsula, and along the east coast. A significant Tamil population is also found in the city of Colombo.

8. The economic problems and limited opportunities of the Kandyans are starkly presented in *Report of the Kandyan Peasantry Commission* (Sessional Paper XVIII, 1951); and N. K. Sarkar and S. J. Tambiah, *The Disintegrating Village* (Colombo: Ceylon University Press Board, 1957).

9. Throughout this study, references to the Tamils without specific indication to the contrary will be to the Ceylon Tamils.

From earliest times, and perhaps before the first Sinhalese arrivals, Dravidian-speaking peoples drifted from South India to Ceylon. Large numbers apparently were absorbed into the Sinhalese population. Certain contemporary Sinhalese castes are thought to have originated in migrations from South India as late as the thirteenth century, followed by adoption of Sinhalese culture and assimilation into the Sinhalese social system as new castes. By about the year 1000, Tamil-speaking people of South Indian origin began to form a distinctive group which did not merge with the Sinhalese population.[10] For some time the Sinhalese and Tamils lived in close physical proximity, but with the decline of a Sinhalese civilization based on Anuradhapura and Polonnaruva by about the thirteenth century, the Sinhalese drifted to the South and West, leaving a vast jungle area with slight population intervening between the two peoples. An independent Tamil kingdom had emerged in the North by this period. Although the culture, language, and customs of both peoples have been influenced by their reciprocal interaction, the island for about 1,000 years has contained two peoples clearly distinguishable by language, religion, and distinctive features of culture and social organization.

Early Tamil migrations are thought to have come principally from the Malabar Coast on the western side of the South Indian peninsula. The people remaining on the Malabar Coast subsequently split off linguistically from the Tamil-speaking people of South India and evolved a separate language of Malayalam. After about the thirteenth century the Coromandel Coast opposite Ceylon increasingly became the source of new Tamil arrivals, but the influence of the early Malabar migrations, as well as long residence in Ceylon and interaction with the Sinhalese, left the Ceylon Tamils as a unique group of Tamil-speaking people, differentiated in customs, speech, and social organization from the Tamils of South India.[11] After the Tamil kingdom in Ceylon was overthrown by the Portuguese at the beginning of the seventeenth century, separate colonial rule tended to retard contacts or a sense of shared experience between the Tamils of Ceylon and India. Both groups were

10. On South Indian migrations and influences, see M. D. Raghavan, *India in Ceylonese History, Society and Culture* (Bombay: Asia Publishing House, 1964); and K. K. Pillay, *South India and Ceylon* (Madras: University of Madras, 1963).

11. S. Arasaratnam, *Ceylon* (Englewood Cliffs, N.J.: Prentice-Hall, Inc., 1964), pp. 102-108.

under British rule from the end of the eighteenth century, but the almost immediate administrative division of Ceylon from British India caused the Ceylon Tamils to look to Colombo for roads, schools, law courts, or government employment and emphasized their involvement in Ceylon and separation from India.

The long-standing concentration of the Tamil community in the northern and eastern portions of the island and Sinhalese numerical predominance throughout the rest of the island have led to the identification of each community with a traditional territory and for many centuries minimized contacts between members of the two communities. A marked territorial concentration has remained to the present day. Tamils continue to constitute more than 95 per cent of the population of the Jaffna District, while Sinhalese form 80 per cent or more of the population in much of the West and South. However, the extensive and rapid development of transportation and communication, the growth of non-agricultural employment, and greater geographical mobility in modern times have produced an appreciable and significant rise in the territorial intermingling of communities. At the census of 1911, the first to distinguish between Ceylon and Indian Tamils, 14.8 per cent of the Ceylon Tamil population lived outside the Northern and Eastern Provinces. By 1953, this proportion had climbed to 23.6 per cent. Sinhalese constituted only 1.8 per cent of the population in the Northern and Eastern Provinces in 1911, but formed 6.6 per cent in 1953. In these years, Tamils had become a proportionally larger element in the population of twelve of fifteen administrative districts outside the Northern and Eastern Provinces, and the Sinhalese proportion of the population had increased in all five districts of the North and East.[12] As the sharp territorial separation of the Sinhalese and Tamils has declined, the increasing contact between the two communities apparently has produced a substantially greater awareness of each other, probably tending to heighten the self-consciousness and reinforce the solidarity and cohesion of each community.

The Indian Tamils are a sizable element in the population of the island but are not accepted as a permanent part of the Ceylonese people

12. Denham, *Ceylon at the Census of 1911*, pp. 197-199, Tables B, C, and D; Ceylon, Department of Census and Statistics, *Census of Ceylon, 1953*, I (Colombo: Government Press, 1957), 178-183, Tables 16 and 17.

and are largely excluded from participation in the political life of Ceylon. The descendants of Tamil-speaking South Indians who migrated to Ceylon as estate laborers in the nineteenth and twentieth centuries, they live primarily on the tea and rubber estates of the interior hill country. In some areas of the hill country, estates populated by Indian Tamils are interspersed among villages of Sinhalese. Elsewhere, particularly in parts of the Nuwara Eliya District and Uva Province, where climate and terrain are inhospitable to traditional patterns of village cultivation, most of the population consists of Indian Tamils. For many decades the estate workers came to Ceylon as temporary sojourners in search of employment, driven by poverty and landlessness from their ancestral villages in South India. They commonly left their families in India and regularly returned to their native villages. Most of the present Indian Tamil population was born in Ceylon and has gradually lost its ties with India. Nonetheless, the Indian Tamils continue to be looked upon as foreigners without an enduring connection or legitimate interest in the island. Hostility toward the Indian Tamils is particularly intense among the Kandyan Sinhalese in those areas where the estates have crowded the villages and Indian labor has restricted the employment opportunities of Sinhalese as population pressure has mounted.

Immediately after independence most Indian Tamils were excluded from Ceylonese citizenship and the franchise. As they were not automatically accepted as citizens of India, most of them became stateless persons. By 1964, 134,000 Indian Tamils, slightly more than one-tenth of the community, had obtained Ceylonese citizenship.[13] Late in that year an agreement was negotiated between Ceylon and India concerning the estimated 975,000 persons of recent Indian origin who were recognized as citizens of neither state. Under the agreement, 525,000 were to be returned to India over a fifteen-year period, and 300,000 were to be granted Ceylonese citizenship and allowed to remain on the island. The fate of the remaining 150,000 was left for later settlement.[14] Although subsequent developments have created uncertainty as to its implementation, the agreement indicates the weak position and uncertain future of the Indian Tamils in Ceylon. It also suggests that a considerable body of Indian Tamils, even if less than half of the present com-

13. *Ceylon Today*, XIII, 2 (Feb., 1964), 19.
14. *Ibid.*, XIII, 11 (Nov., 1964), 15-22.

munity, is likely to become a permanent part of the population. Largely isolated on the estates, possessing almost no middle class, economically weak, and educationally backward, the Indian Tamils were seldom
prominent in public affairs, and the political role of the community declined further with their virtual exclusion from the polity after independence.

The other communities of Ceylon are considerably smaller. The island's Muslims are divided into three separate communities. The Ceylon
Moors form less than 6 per cent of the population. The name Moor was
applied to Ceylonese Muslims by the Portuguese in the sixteenth century
and has remained in use. Islam was first brought to Ceylon by Arab traders, and the modern Moor community claims an Arabic origin. It is highly probable that the community today is a product of considerable intermarriage between Arab traders and Sinhalese or Tamils and was substantially enlarged by migrations of Indian Muslims. The Moors for
the most part have adopted Tamil as the language of the home. Orig-
inally concentrated on the south and west coasts, the Moors sought to
escape Portuguese persecution early in the seventeenth century by mi-
grating in considerable numbers to the interior and the east coast, then
under control of the King of Kandy. An important concentration of
Moors remains on the east coast south of Batticaloa, where they have
taken up agriculture. Moors are numerous in the cities of Colombo and
Kandy and north of Colombo on the west coast. In addition, many
members of the community are scattered through the island, frequently
as merchants and traders. The Indian Moors are more recent Muslim
immigrants from India. They include many urban laborers and small
traders and a few prosperous Colombo businessmen. The third Muslim
community is the small group called Malays, the descendants of East
Indian troops brought to Ceylon by the Dutch. The Malays have tended
to remain concentrated in the army, police, and other government
employment.

The very small Burgher community, only one-half of 1 per cent of
the island's population, is of mixed Ceylonese and European ancestry.
Although the term Burgher is a product of Dutch rule, it is used to
refer to persons with Portuguese as well as Dutch antecedents. The
Burghers are almost entirely urban and Christian. Despite the small
size of their community, they played a prominent part in the island's

affairs during the colonial period and for some time predominated in the public service and professions.

Modern communalism in Ceylon is characterized by its political role. Communal rivalry in recent decades has closely followed the emergence of a popular-based, participant political process. In Ceylon as elsewhere in Southern Asia, release from colonial rule and creation of a modern state seem to have stimulated communal and other particularistic sentiments by providing a new arena for competition and a more valuable prize for which to compete.[15] The existing sentiments of communal identification and solidarity have been used to mobilize political support by prospects of gaining satisfactions for the community and its members through state action. Communalist sentiments do not appear to be as conspicuously aggressive, competitive, and exclusive in other spheres of behavior. Relations between communities seem normally to have been relaxed and marked by little if any overt hostility, although they have tended to be somewhat restrained and impersonal, and there are indications of latent unfavorable attitudes by members of each community toward the other.[16] Heightened antagonisms and eruptions of communal violence in 1956 and 1958 followed the excitement of communal passions by intense political agitation and resort to communal appeals in competition for political support. Except for these periods of communal violence, the seeming paradox has existed of amicable relations among members of different communities, readily observable at the lowest levels of interaction in the everyday lives of ordinary Ceylonese, at the same time that the communities appear to be locked in mortal struggle in the political sphere.

The most significant political rivalry has been between the Sinhalese majority and the Ceylon Tamil minority. With universal suffrage and mass political participation, the Moors, Malays, and Burghers are too small in number and too scattered for serious political competition. The Indian Tamils suffer from disabilities which have severely restricted the part they have been able to play in politics. In political terms, the

15. See Geertz, "The Integrative Revolution," p. 120.

16. Some of the unfortunately meager existing evidence on Sinhalese and Tamil perceptions of each other is discussed in T. L. Green, "Research in the Social Sciences in Ceylon University, Colombo," *International Social Science Bulletin*, III, 4 (Winter, 1951), 832-842; and W. Howard Wriggins, *Ceylon: Dilemmas of a New Nation* (Princeton: Princeton University Press, 1960), pp. 231-233.

communal situation in Ceylon is a relatively uncomplicated one of a single community with an overwhelming majority facing a much smaller minority clearly defined by language, religion, and territorial concentration. Since independence, the most critical problem that has pitted the Sinhalese against the Tamils and raised unambiguous communal issues has been the official language question. This issue has come to symbolize to the Sinhalese their aspirations to retrieve their ancestral heritage and reassert their position and prerogatives as the majority, which they felt were denied them under colonial rule. To the Tamils, the language issue has symbolized the dread domination of the Sinhalese majority and threatened their existence as a separate group. The official language problem precipitated the most serious confrontation of communities in modern times.

Language probably is the most important single attribute delimiting each community.[17] Language has been both a source of emotional identification within each community and a communications barrier between communities. Although there are a few exceptions, the connection between the speakers of the language and the members of the community is extremely close. It is significant that for both communities the language and the people are identified by the same name. For the Sinhalese, the maintenance of an Aryan language for more than 2,000 years although surrounded by Dravidian-speaking peoples has contributed to and is indicative of the strong sense of Sinhalese group self-identification.

The language difference has formed an obvious obstacle to integration by hindering communications and tending to compartmentalize the two communities.[18] In 1953, 80 per cent of the population of Ceylon

17. Jennings has persuasively argued that the Sinhalese and Tamils are essentially language groups. Nearly a decade before the official language controversy produced a serious rupture between communities, he cited language as the "foundation of communalism as it developed in Ceylon." Sir W. Ivor Jennings, "Communalism and the New Constitution" (article reprinted as a leaflet, from the *Hindu Organ*, Dec. 10, 1945), p. 5. On the political difficulties created by linguistic diversity in the newly independent states of Asia and Africa, see Rupert Emerson, *From Empire to Nation: The Rise to Self-Assertion of Asian and African Peoples* (Boston: Beacon Press, 1960), pp. 132-148.

18. The vital role of effective and swift communication over a wide range of subjects in the development of cohesion and unity among peoples has been emphasized by Karl W. Deutsch, *Nationalism and Social Communication* (Cambridge, Mass.: M.I.T. Press, 1953), esp. pp. 60-74.

Table 4. *Languages spoken by Ceylon population three years of age and over, 1953*

Language(s) spoken[a]	Number	Percentage of population three years of age and over
Sinhalese only	4,289,957	58.9
Tamil only	1,570,084	21.6
English only	14,066	0.2
Sinhalese and Tamil	719,194	9.9
Sinhalese and English	307,570	4.2
Tamil and English	146,549	2.0
Sinhalese, Tamil, and English	233,567	3.2
	7,280,987	100.0

[a]The ability to speak a language was defined as "the ability to conduct a short conversation, or understand and answer questions put in that language."
Source: Ceylon, Department of Census and Statistics, *Census of Ceylon, 1953*, Vol. III, Part I (Colombo: Government Press, 1960), p. 604, Table 17.

spoke only one language. Nearly 60 per cent spoke only Sinhalese and more than 20 per cent spoke only Tamil. Both Sinhalese and Tamil were spoken by only about 13 per cent of the population (see Table 4). The language barrier has meant that Sinhalese attend schools conducted in Sinhalese, read Sinhalese-language newspapers, and listen to Sinhalese-language radio broadcasts, while Tamils are exposed to separate Tamil-language experiences. Thus, in 1964 the first newspaper readership survey to be conducted in Ceylon found that the reading of publications in more than one language was limited to a very small proportion of the population, almost entirely of the urban middle class. The survey found that while 53 per cent of the men and 23 per cent of the women read some publication, 42 per cent of the men and 16 per cent of the women read only Sinhalese publications, 3 per cent of the men and 1 per cent of the women read only Tamil publications, and 3 per cent of the men and 4 per cent of the women read only English publications. Only 4 per cent of the men and 3 per cent of the women read both English and Sinhalese publications, and less than one-half of 1 per cent of the men and no detectable proportion of the women read both English and Tamil publications. The reading of both Sinhalese and Tamil publications was almost non-existent.[19]

19. A few members of the urban middle class read Sinhalese, Tamil, and English publications, but their number was too small (constituting 1 per cent of urban upper-

The separation of communities resulting from language differences has been reduced somewhat, however, by the centralized control of education and communications media in the Sinhalese, Tamil, and English languages by the same government departments and publishing firms. Radio programs broadcast in all three languages, for example, are a part of the National Service of Radio Ceylon, which is operated as a government department. Most large circulation Sinhalese and Tamil newspapers are published by companies which also produce newspapers in the other languages. Communication between communities in public affairs has been and remains in the hands of English-educated community leaders, who often communicate more fluently with each other in English than with the people of their own community who do not know English.

This study is an attempt to examine the impact of communalism on politics in contemporary Ceylon. The study is concerned with the relations between the majority Sinhalese community and the principal minority, the Ceylon Tamil community. Other communities are discussed only incidentally as they enter into the Sinhalese-Tamil competition. After tracing the pre-independence growth of communal rivalry as political reforms led toward a competitive majoritarian political process and self-government, the study devotes particular attention to the official language controversy, which has been the principal issue of contention between Sinhalese and Tamil peoples and has dominated communal relations since shortly after independence. The official language question strikingly illustrates the fundamental problems of communities and communalism in a newly created state striving to establish a modern democratic civil order, and is therefore a convenient device for illuminating the role of communalism in Ceylonese politics.

---

middle-class men) to be detected in the islandwide results. "Readership Survey, Ceylon, April-June 1964, Conducted for the Audit Bureau of Circulations Limited by the Market Research Department of Lever Brothers (Ceylon) Limited" (mimeographed; Colombo, Sept., 1964), Table 17.

CHAPTER I

Communal relations and social and political change

The compartmentalization of the people of Ceylon into distinct ethnic communities antedated the long and profound Western impact on the island and still existed at the conclusion of more than four centuries of Western rule. The social, economic, and political changes of the colonial period had major consequences for the nature of communal relations, however. The three centuries of Portuguese and Dutch involvement on the island from 1505 to 1798, when the Dutch were succeeded by the British as rulers of the coastal areas, produced relatively modest dislocations of the social relationships and patterns of life of most Ceylonese. In contrast, the nineteenth century saw the beginning of major changes which eventually were to touch the life of virtually every person on the island. In the course of the century a transformation from a static, traditional society to a more flexible, modernizing society commenced. The tremendous impact colonial rule and Western influences were to have in the nineteenth and twentieth centuries reflected not simply a change in colonial masters from Dutch to British but the great industrial, social, and ideological changes occurring in Europe and particularly in Britain in that period.

Reforms in 1833 undermined the feudal system of service obligations and land tenure and led to greater uniformity in the administration of the island.[1] The introduction of plantation agriculture at mid-century, initially coffee cultivation which was replaced by tea in the closing decades of the century, produced fundamental changes in the economy of the island. Education after the last decades of the nineteenth century spread from Colombo and a few other cities to all but the most

1. On the reforms of 1833, see G. C. Mendis (ed.), *The Colebrooke-Cameron Papers: Documents on British Colonial Policy in Ceylon, 1796-1833* (2 vols.; London: Oxford University Press, 1956).

remote rural areas and advanced from primary to secondary and eventually to university and professional training. A middle class of public servants, doctors, lawyers, planters, and businessmen developed. The erosion of the feudal basis of society as a result of planned and unplanned government action, the availability of education, the growth of a bureaucracy recruited on the basis of impersonal achievement criteria, and the opening of avenues of social mobility by the economic activity following on the spread of plantation agriculture all contributed to the weakening of the rigid, ascriptive, and hierarchical features of the traditional social order.

Political awakening and the independence movement

The awakening of Ceylonese political consciousness, leading to the emergence of an independence movement, added a political dimension to the relations between communities. From the earliest times, each group lived, or believed itself to live, apart from the other. The periods of warfare between Sinhalese and Tamil kingdoms apparently at times aroused a sense of unity among the Sinhalese, the most notable case being the rallying of the Sinhalese people by Duttugemunu against the rule of the Tamil King Elara in the second century, B.C.[2] Generally, however, the age-old cultural bonds which united members of one community and separated them from members of other communities had little political relevance. Tamils lived under Sinhalese rulers and Sinhalese under Tamil rulers. Tamil influences and courtiers were common in the courts of the Sinhalese kings. The Kandyan Kingdom, the last independent bastion of the Sinhalese people, was ruled for many years before its demise in 1815 by a line of Tamil kings. By the end of the nineteenth century a considerable part of the island, including both Sinhalese and Tamils, had been under common foreign rule for three

2. The story of Duttugemunu's victory over Elara appears in *The Mahāvamsa or the Great Chronicle of Ceylon*, trans. Wilhelm Geiger (London: Oxford University Press, 1912), pp. 170-178. A Sinhalese scholar has recently written of the episode: "The entire Sinhalese race was united under the banner of the young Gamani [Duttugemunu]. This was the beginning of nationalism among the Sinhalese." Walpola Rahula, *History of Buddhism in Ceylon: The Anuradhapura Period* (Colombo: M. D. Gunasena & Co., Ltd., 1956), p. 79. The story has lived throughout Sinhalese history and has become one of the most powerful myths of the Sinhalese.

centuries, and the entire island for nearly a century had lived under a single colonial administration.

At about the same time that the complex and interrelated social, economic, and ideological changes involved in modernization were beginning to gather speed, Ceylonese began to develop the idea that they should have some share in governing Ceylon. With the expectation of Ceylonese self-government, communal attitudes and loyalties became politically significant. The gradual transfer of power from foreign to Ceylonese hands quickly created concern for the relative political strength of the various communities. The basic assumption upon which this concern rested was that the share of political power held by members of one community would be used for the exclusive benefit of that community or to the detriment of other communities. This assumption stemmed from the enduring strength of communal identification and solidarity. The Donoughmore Commission, reviewing the political situation in Ceylon in 1928, warned:

Not only is the population not homogeneous, but the diverse elements of which it is composed distrust and suspect each other. It is almost true to say that the conception of patriotism in Ceylon is as much racial [i.e., communal] as national and that the best interests of the country are at times regarded as synonymous with the welfare of a particular section of its people.[3]

Modern political awareness originated with the appearance of sentiment for the reform of the colonial regime in the direction of Ceylonese self-government. These political stirrings closely followed the emergence of an educated, affluent, and largely urban middle class among the Sinhalese and Tamils late in the nineteenth century. Earlier agitation for reform had been limited to the island's few Europeans and Burghers. For many decades political consciousness and political activity hardly extended beyond this middle class.

The appearance of a Ceylonese middle class characterized by Western education and urban occupations related to the growth of modern bureaucratic, professional, and commercial activity was one of the most significant social consequences of the nineteenth century changes. The far-reaching reforms of 1833 tended to break down restraining feudal

3. Great Britain, Colonial Office, *Ceylon: Report of the Special Commission on the Constitution*, Cmd. 3131 (London: His Majesty's Stationery Office, 1928), p. 31. This report is hereafter cited as Donoughmore Report.

relationships and facilitate geographical and occupational mobility. The spread of planting in the second half of the century was accompanied by the rapid construction of roads and railroads and an acceleration of the pace of economic activity. Business firms were established, and the public service underwent a considerable expansion, multiplying opportunities for urban white-collar employment. Near the end of the century, Ceylonese began to climb to the higher levels of the bureaucracy and increasingly to enter the expanding professions.[4] Among the early entrants into urban administrative or professional occupations were the sons of the Sinhalese low-country Mudaliyars, a traditional land-holding aristocracy, and the landed gentry, who were among the first to obtain Western educations.[5] By the beginning of the present century, trade, transportation, contracting, mining, and planting had contributed to the emergence of a fairly sizable group of modestly wealthy Low-Country Sinhalese. Graphite mining and coconut planting, which had been prospering, were almost entirely under Ceylonese ownership and management. A description of Ceylon at the beginning of the century noted the existence of "a very large number of wealthy native gentlemen enriched by trade and agriculture within British times."[6] The newly affluent families commonly used their resources to provide their sons

4. For the developments in nineteenth-century Ceylon, see I. H. Vanden Driesen, "Some Trends in the Economic History of Ceylon in the 'Modern' Period," *Ceylon Journal of Historical and Social Studies*, III, 1 (Jan.-June, 1960), 1-17; G. C. Mendis, *Ceylon Under the British* (2nd ed. rev.; Colombo: Colombo Apothecaries Co., Ltd., 1948); and S. G. Perera, S.J., *A History of Ceylon*, Vol. II: *The British Period and After, 1796-1956*, rev. by V. Perniola, S.J. (7th ed.; Colombo: Associated Newspapers of Ceylon, Ltd., 1959).

5. Because these aristocratic or quasi-aristocratic elements combined with groups thrusting upward from less prestigious traditional statuses in the formation of the urban middle class, the new social formation is sometimes referred to as the "middle and upper classes." For convenience here, the entire group, irrespective of position of origin in the traditional social hierarchy, will be termed simply the "middle class." After the period under discussion, an increasingly significant differentiation developed between the university-educated professionals and higher public servants, on the one hand, and, on the other, the clerical and other intermediate-level employees whose English educations stopped at the secondary level. The terms "upper-middle class" and "lower-middle class" are commonly employed to distinguish these two socio-economic levels. A survey of the structure and ideology of the middle class is contained in S. J. Tambiah, "Ceylon," in Richard D. Lambert and Bert F. Hoselitz (eds.), *The Role of Savings and Wealth in Southern Asia and the West* (Paris: UNESCO, 1963), pp. 55-61. For a sketch of the growth of the middle class, see Ralph Pieris, "New Elites in Ceylon," in *Transactions of the Fifth World Congress of Sociology* (Louvain, Belgium: International Sociological Association, 1964), III, 295-302.

6. John Ferguson, *Ceylon in 1903* (Colombo: A. M. & J. Ferguson, 1903), p. 85.

with Western education in preparation for careers in the public service or professions and to buy land, thus perpetuating their economic and social advance.

The emerging middle class cut across the traditional lines of social stratification imbedded in a hierarchical ordering of castes.[7] While the significance of caste as an endogamous and solidary social group did not vanish, the appearance of the middle class created a new form of stratification based on wealth, education, and occupation rather than ascribed status. Alongside members of the traditionally dominant and numerically largest Goyigama (cultivator) caste were relatively numerous representatives of other castes ranking lower on the ritual hierarchy. Among those most intimately involved in the late nineteenth-century growth of entrepreneurial activity and changing social patterns were members of the Karāva (fisher), Salāgama (cinnamon peeler), and Durāva (toddy tapper) castes of the southwest coastal areas. Many of the traders, contractors, and craftsmen for the new economic activity were provided by these low-country castes. Some individuals belonging to the Karāva caste in particular were notably successful in commerce and amassed considerable wealth. Not only trade and planting but appointments in the government service and careers in the law courts had begun to open to these castes with the establishment of schools by Christian missionary groups and the government in the Southwest. Through their growing economic power, they were able at times to challenge the social and political dominance of the Goyigama caste. In 1912, the Goyigama monopoly of Legislative Council seats was broken with the nomination of a member of the Karāva caste to the council. The low-country castes were to provide a considerable share of the leadership of the movement for self-government.

The rise of the middle class is intimately connected with the expansion of education in English, which gained momentum in the last decades of the nineteenth century. The increasingly available urban white-collar careers universally required literacy in English, the language of government and commerce. Both Low-Country Sinhalese and Tamils flocked to English schools and the occupations requiring knowl-

---

7. The Sinhalese caste system and the changes it has undergone are described in Bryce Ryan, *Caste in Modern Ceylon* (New Brunswick, N.J.: Rutgers University Press, 1953).

edge of English. By 1911, 3.3 per cent of the population of the island was literate in English. In the cities of Colombo and Kandy, between 17 and 20 per cent of the men and more than 10 per cent of the women were English literates. Excluding Europeans, Burghers, and Eurasians, nearly 71,000 Ceylonese were able to read and write the English language.[8]

The avenues of social mobility provided by commerce, planting, transport, and mining by which the Low-Country Sinhalese climbed into the middle class were not available to the Tamils of the North. Consequently, for the Tamils, English education and bureaucratic and other white-collar employment played a proportionately greater role in social movement than for the Sinhalese. Thrift, diligence, or inherited land ownership, and the early establishment of Christian missionary schools in the North enabled certain Tamil families to secure English educations for their sons, who were therefore able to enter the bureaucracy, commercial establishments, or the professions, mostly in the South.[9] The incomes thus earned combined with the dowries attracted by favorable occupational prospects became the basis for a claim to middle-class status.

The middle class which was thus developing was characterized by mobility upward on the social ladder, from the village to the city, and from a traditional toward a Western culture and value system. The English-educated middle class remained small and exclusive in relation to the total population,[10] a circumstance which was to be a later source of social and political discontent. The immediate political consequence of the formation of this class, however, was the demand for Ceylonese participation in government.

Between 1833 and 1912, the governmental institutions of Ceylon had changed little. Government was completely autocratic, although increasingly aspiring to be paternalistic and benevolent. Authority was

8. E. B. Denham, *Ceylon at the Census of 1911* (Colombo: Government Printer, 1912), pp. 433-436. For a discussion of English education and the formation of the middle class, see Ralph Pieris, "Universities, Politics and Public Opinion in Ceylon," *Minerva*, II, 4 (Summer, 1964), 435-444.

9. See S. J. Tambiah, "Ethnic Representation in Ceylon's Higher Administrative Services, 1870-1946," *University of Ceylon Review*, XIII, 2-3 (April-July, 1955), 129-131.

10. Jennings estimated the middle class shortly before independence at under 5 per cent of the population. Sir W. Ivor Jennings, *The Economy of Ceylon* (2nd ed.; London: Oxford University Press, 1951), p. 13.

concentrated in the hands of colonial officials headed by the governor. There was little communication between ruler and ruled. After 1833, unofficial members were appointed to the Legislative Council to reflect various opinions within the population. Until 1889, three Ceylonese— a Sinhalese, a Tamil, and a Burgher—and three Europeans composed the unofficial minority of the council. The first Sinhalese and Tamil unofficial members appointed to the council were, respectively, the chief interpreter of the Supreme Court and the interpreter for the revenue commissioner. Commencing in 1889, Ceylonese representation on the council was increased to five. With two exceptions after 1912, the Ceylonese representatives continued to be appointed by the governor, and the majority of official members was maintained until 1920. In any case, executive authority was firmly held by the governor. After 1912, constitutional changes came rapidly, with increasing opportunity for participation by Ceylonese and articulation of Ceylonese aspirations. In two decades Ceylon passed politically from colonial absolutism almost devoid of Ceylonese participation to a wide measure of internal self-government through representative institutions based on universal adult suffrage. In less than four decades Ceylon had become a fully independent state.

The desire for political reform was greatly stimulated by the government's handling of rioting between Sinhalese and Muslims in 1915. The government, appearing to be remarkably out of touch with the population and uneasy because of the war in Europe, declared martial law and resorted to severe measures of repression. A number of persons were summarily executed, and many prominent Sinhalese were arrested. The response of the colonial officials to the riots not only tarnished the image of the British government as a bulwark of justice and liberty but starkly illuminated the weaknesses of articulation between the colonial government and the Ceylonese people. The episode apparently led many to accept the necessity of representative institutions and Ceylonese control of the government.[11]

11. A graphic and poignant portrayal of the events by a prominent Ceylonese is contained in P. [Sir Ponnambalam] Ramanathan, *Riots and Martial Law in Ceylon, 1915* (London: St. Martin's Press, 1916). On the role of the suppression of the riots in creating pressure for political reform, see *ibid.*, pp. 58-60; D. C. Vijayavardhana, *The Revolt in the Temple* (Colombo: Sinha Publications, 1953), p. 128; and Joint Committee of the Ceylon National Association and the Ceylon Reform League, "Case for Constitutional Reform in Ceylon," in S. W. R. D. Bandaranaike (ed.), *The Handbook*

The growing sentiment for political reform and a greater Ceylonese voice in the government of the colony, which eventually was extended to the demand for independence, led to organized activity shortly after the turn of the century. The Ceylon Agricultural Association, formed during the preceding century, was transformed into the Ceylon National Association and began to press for political reform in the first decade of the twentieth century. It was joined by the Ceylon Reform League in 1917, and the two organizations combined to form the Ceylon National Congress in 1919.[12] The Congress and its predecessors were composed almost entirely of Westernized middle-class, English-educated Ceylonese, frequently lawyers, planters, businessmen, and retired public service officers, most of whom belonged to moderately wealthy property-owning families. A colonial governor, in dismissing one of the early arguments for liberalization of the colony's government, declared in a dispatch to London that the agitation emanated from "those of the natives of Ceylon who have assimilated an education of a purely Western, as opposed to Oriental, type, and who are to be regarded, not as representative Ceylonese, but as a product of the European administration of Ceylon on lines approved by British tradition."[13] At the inaugural meeting of the Congress, the organization's newly elected president confided: "To me the Congress is the fulfillment of dreams cherished from the time I was an undergraduate at Cambridge."[14] The second president of the Congress was also a Cambridge graduate, the first Asian to be elected president of the Cambridge Union. Of the Congress's first eight presidents, one had completed a distinguished career in the exclusive Ceylon Civil Service, five were lawyers, one was a rubber planter, and one, Sir Baron Jayatilaka, although of humble origin, was a teacher and scholar who earned an Oxford degree and studied law in Britain.

The Congress and the independence movement remained the al-

of the *Ceylon National Congress, 1919-1928* (Colombo: H. W. Cave & Co., 1928), p. 167.

12. On the origin and early period of the movement for self-government, see Bandaranaike, *Handbook of the Ceylon National Congress*, esp. pp. 177, 282-284; and H. A. J. Hulugalle, *The Life and Times of D. R. Wijewardene* (Colombo: Associated Newspapers of Ceylon, Ltd., 1960), pp. 60-77, 115-122.

13. Dispatch from Governor Sir Henry McCallum to the Earl of Crewe, in Bandaranaike, *Handbook of the Ceylon National Congress*, p. 48.

14. Sir Ponnambalam Arunachalam, Presidential Address, *ibid.*, p. 194.

most exclusive preserve of the middle class throughout the colonial period. In marked contrast to the independence struggle led by the Indian National Congress, into which Gandhi injected characteristics of a mass popular movement early in the present century, the Ceylonese independence movement failed to establish roots or engender enthusiasm among the masses. The Congress, dominated by lawyers and men of property, was cautious and conservative, pledging to achieve its goal "by constitutional methods by a reform of the existing system of Government and Administration."[15] The middle-class conservatism of the Congress was illustrated in 1927 when the organization argued for the retention of a limited franchise based on an income qualification in preference to the major enlargement of the suffrage which was under consideration.[16] Progress toward independence came steadily and without conflict, if not always as swiftly as was desired. The kind of heroic struggle which might have aroused popular emotions and rapidly kindled mass political consciousness did not occur.

Early in the life of the movement for political autonomy, some hope and expectation existed that the struggle for Ceylonese self-government would unify the Sinhalese and Tamils in a common cause. The politically active middle class was multi-communal in composition and relatively cosmopolitan in outlook. The English language formed a strong bond among middle-class members of the two communities. In the English-language schools, the public service, the British-owned commercial and financial establishments, and the law courts, Sinhalese and Tamils studied, worked, or pleaded side by side in English. Command of English also tended to separate them from the vernacular-speaking members of their own communities. Urbanization created residential intermingling of Sinhalese and Tamil families. While even within this class, communal identity was not obliterated and marriage seldom leaped communal barriers, relations between Sinhalese and Tamils were not only free of tension but were often cordial and warm. It was a sign of "modernity" to reject communal sentiments as barbarous and atavistic. How many silently retained attitudes of communal exclusiveness existed behind a public façade of cosmopolitanism is problematical. Un-

---

15. "Constitution of the Ceylon National Congress," *ibid.*, Appendix H, p. 162.
16. See "Evidence Given by the Representatives of the Ceylon National Congress before the Special Commission at the Town Hall, Colombo on 22nd and 23rd November, 1927," *ibid.*, pp. 829-830.

questionably, however, close and friendly social and professional contacts between middle-class Sinhalese and Tamils were and have continued to be common. It has been in the field of politics, particularly as the necessity arose to seek progressively wider popular support, that relations between communities have been subjected to severe strains.

A few initial signs of Sinhalese-Tamil unity in the struggle for political reform appeared. A constitutional revision in 1912 provided for the election of a member of the Legislative Council on a very narrow franchise consisting of the Western-educated Ceylonese (excluding Burghers). In this election, a Tamil candidate, Sir Ponnambalam Ramanathan, defeated a Sinhalese candidate and became the first Ceylonese elected to public office[17] and the first non-communal representative on the council. Ramanathan's brother, Sir Ponnambalam Arunachalam, was the first president of the Ceylon Reform League and became the first president of the Ceylon National Congress when that organization was launched in 1919. His successor as president declared to the Congress: "The past few years have shown us that the Sinhalese and the Tamils are one people (cheers). This struggle we are entering today will cement that union stronger and stronger."[18]

The frailty of the proclaimed unity of Sinhalese and Tamils was quickly demonstrated, however. Only two years after the founding of the Congress a rupture occurred between its principal Sinhalese and Tamil members. In 1921, Sir Ponnambalam Arunachalam, the former president, and most of the other Tamil congressmen left the organization in a disagreement over their demand for a reserved Tamil seat in the Legislative Council to represent the Tamil minority in the predominantly Sinhalese Western Province. The unwillingness of several leading Sinhalese congressmen to accept Arunachalam as a candidate for the City of Colombo seat on the council is thought to have contributed to the break.[19] Arunachalam and his brother Ramanathan formed

17. A Burgher and two Europeans were chosen by communal electorates at the same time.

18. Sir James Pieris, Presidential Address, in Bandaranaike, *Handbook of the Ceylon National Congress*, p. 237.

19. See *ibid.*, pp. 339-360, 394, 644-646; Hulugalle, *Life and Times of D. R. Wijewardene*, pp. 121-122; and Great Britain, Colonial Office, *Further Correspondence Relating to the Revision of the Constitution of Ceylon*, Cmd. 2062 (London: His Majesty's Stationery Office, 1924), pp. 6-7. The reserved Tamil seat in the Western Province was granted in 1924, and Sir Ponnambalam Ramanathan was elected to it.

an organization called the Tamil Maha Jana Sabha to speak for the political interests of the Tamils. While a few individual Tamils remained within the Congress, it became primarily an organization of Low-Country Sinhalese. The authority of the Congress to speak for Ceylonese political aspirations suffered from the exodus of the Tamils and the Congress never developed the following or prestige of the Indian National Congress, although it remained one of the few significant political organizations until independence a quarter century later.

Almost at its inception, the independence movement split on communal lines. The integrative forces that had developed in the preceding years were not strong enough to overcome the communal sense of separate interests and the suspicions created by communal consciousness. The split was a triumph of primordial identification and loyalty over the new identifications based on class, urbanization, and Westernization. The Tamil departure from the Congress marked the beginning of the rivalry between Sinhalese and Tamils which, although seldom bitter and never violent, became a persistent feature of the transition to independence.

Political reform and communal rivalry

In its first years the fledgling independence movement stressed Sinhalese-Tamil unity in opposition to a skeptical colonial regime. Increasingly thereafter, advance toward self-government was accompanied by Sinhalese-Tamil rivalry. The period from 1920 to 1946 was one of perpetual constitution-writing. Scarcely was one constitution in effect before the design of its successor was mooted. New constitutions appeared in 1920, 1924, 1931, and 1946. The latter with some modifications became the constitution of independent Ceylon. The 1931 constitution had the longest life, but demands for its revision commenced in its first year. The constant debate of constitutional questions, the progressive extension of internal autonomy, and the increasing popular control of government stimulated communal fears and suspicions, particularly among the minorities.

In a famous memorandum drafted for the secretary of state for the colonies in 1908, James Pieris, later the second president of the Ceylon National Congress, singled out as the two urgently needed political reforms "the abolition of the present system of racial representation, and the introduction of the elective principle in place of nomination."[20] Until the second decade of the twentieth century, representation had been entirely on a communal basis and by nomination of the governor. From 1833 to 1889, three Europeans, a Sinhalese, a Tamil, and a Burgher were nominated to the Legislative Council to represent their respective communities. In 1889, a second Sinhalese to represent the Kandyans and a Muslim were added. The entering wedge of non-communal and elective representation came with the 1912 "educated Ceylonese" seat on the council, although six other council members continued to be nominated and three elected on the basis of community. The 1920 and 1924 constitutions combined territorial with communal representation and election with nomination. Eleven territorial electorates were created by the 1920 constitution. In addition, two Europeans and a Burgher were elected on a communally restricted franchise and representatives were selected by the Chamber of Commerce and the Low-Country Products Association, the former European and the latter largely Low-Country Sinhalese in membership. Under the 1924 constitution, twenty-three council members were elected from territorial constituencies and eleven from communal constituencies, with three additional members appointed to represent "other interests."[21]

The final abandonment of communal representation and the complete triumph of popular election were products of a commission under the chairmanship of the Earl of Donoughmore charged with recommending constitutional revision. In its report issued in 1928, the Donoughmore Commission denounced communal representation in uncompromising terms, charging that it had been a barrier to communal harmony and co-operation and that "only by its abolition will it be possible for the various diverse communities to develop together a true national unity."[22] The 1931 constitution based on the Donoughmore pro-

20. The text of the memorandum appears in Bandaranaike, *Handbook of the Ceylon National Congress*, pp. 6-16.

21. A summary of the Legislative Council reforms is contained in Perera, *A History of Ceylon*, Vol. II, chap. vii.

22. Donoughmore Report, pp. 90-101. In a frequently cited passage, the report described communal representation as "a cancer on the body politic, eating deeper and deeper into the vital energies of the people, breeding self-interest, suspicion and animosity, poisoning the new growth of political consciousness, and effectively preventing the development of a national or corporate spirit." *Ibid.*, p. 39.

posals created a State Council consisting of sixty-one members, fifty of whom were elected from territorial constituencies with populations as nearly equal as was feasible. The remaining members included eight persons appointed by the governor to represent interests deemed inadequately represented and three senior officers of the colonial administration. Except for the appointed members, some of whom represented interests other than communal, representation on the basis of community disappeared. A more dramatic innovation was the commission's recommendation for broadening of the suffrage. Despite an almost total absence of support for universal suffrage among Ceylonese politicians, the commission suggested an extension of the franchise which, when slightly enlarged by the Colonial Office, made Ceylon the first country in Asia to introduce universal adult suffrage. The number of registered voters jumped from 205,000 (about 4 per cent of the population) in 1924 to more than 1.5 million (nearly 30 per cent of the total population) in 1931.[23]

The Donoughmore Constitution was a major landmark in Ceylonese political development. It made possible for the first time a Ceylonese political process based on wide popular participation. Although the government of the island had been liberalized gradually over the preceding two decades to allow a greater Ceylonese voice, the suffrage was sharply restricted and the governor and officials responsible to him retained effective control of the government. With the Donoughmore Constitution, Ceylon obtained a large degree of internal autonomy exercised through a chamber predominantly chosen by universal suffrage from territorial constituencies.

The implications of these developments for communal relations were obvious. The reforms since 1920 had tended to enhance the political strength of the Sinhalese majority relative to the Tamil minority. As the Sinhalese constituted some two-thirds of the island's population, with the advent of universal suffrage a preponderance of territorial

23. The number of registered voters in 1931 apparently fell considerably short of the number of persons legally eligible to vote with the grant of universal adult suffrage, as political consciousness seeped into the rural villages only gradually during the next two decades. Nonetheless, with the extension of the franchise the effective electorate underwent an abrupt sevenfold increase. The figures on registered voters are from Great Britain, Colonial Office, *Ceylon: Report of the Commission on Constitutional Reform*, Cmd. 6677 (London: His Majesty's Stationery Office, 1945), p. 54. This report is hereafter cited as Soulbury Report.

constituencies were bound to contain a majority of Sinhalese voters. With the political advances, the Sinhalese majority in the population was increasingly able to assert its strength politically. In the debates on constitutional revision after 1920, the Sinhalese, with the confidence and security of superior numbers, could insist on the simple and familiar devices of democratic government—territorial constituencies and equal representation for equal populations—without reference to communal consequences. The Sinhalese reliance on majoritarianism and exaspera- tion with minority resistance were voiced with a candor not typical for the period by the president of the Ceylon National Congress in 1921:

> [With territorial constituencies] it is by no means certain that for a place like Colombo or even the Provinces the elected man would be necessarily a Sinhalese. But suppose he is a Sinhalese? What then? Why should he not be elected? Why should there not be a majority of the men whom the electors think should be elected? Is there anything wrong in the Sinhalese man that he should not be in a majority? . . . It is the electors' choice, and he [sic] is free to choose. "But," say our wiseacres, "if he is elected and if you have an elected majority that elected majority will rule." Why should not they? (Applause). Who is to rule them? The minority?[24]

If the belief had been prevalent that ethnic and linguistic differences were irrelevant to the issues confronting a modern state, no reason would have existed for disputing the claims of majority rule. However, the expectation of solidarity within and competition between communi- ties on political questions was clearly evident, particularly among those who spoke for the Tamil community. This expectation led the Tamils to seek some means of curbing the potential power of the Sinhalese majority. As a minority barely one-sixth as numerous as the Sinhalese, the Tamils would be perpetually at the mercy of the Sinhalese if no deviation occurred from the principle of majority rule. The small Burgher and Moor communities, which along with the Europeans had been the chief beneficiaries of the earlier representation on a communal basis, were the most insistent advocates of communal representation, which they considered essential for them to retain any voice in politics.[25] The concentration of Tamil population in the North and East assured

24. H. J. C. Pereira, Presidential Address, in Bandaranaike, *Handbook of the Ceylon National Congress*, p. 356.
25. See Great Britain, Colonial Office, *Correspondence Regarding the Constitution of Ceylon*, Cmd. 3419 (London: His Majesty's Stationery Office, 1929), pp. 19-20.

the Tamils of representation from territorial constituencies, and in the early days of the movement for political reform Tamils had joined in the denunciation of representation based on community.[26] However, as their concern over the enhanced political strength of the Sinhalese mounted, Tamil leaders supported selective use of communal representation and sought other devices to curtail the political power of the Sinhalese.

In the early 1920's an agreement was reached between the leaders of the Ceylon National Congress and the Tamil leadership for a ratio of one Tamil to two Sinhalese representatives, which was the result produced by the 1924 constitution.[27] Tamil pronouncements to the Donoughmore Commission appealed for the retention of this ratio, which with the representation of other minorities deprived the Sinhalese of an absolute majority in the legislative chamber. The commission rejected outright the idea of fixing relative proportions of Sinhalese and Tamil legislative seats and proposed an essentially majoritarian scheme with territorial constituencies of approximately equal population.[28] In the 1931 State Council the Sinhalese for the first time obtained an absolute legislative majority over the representatives of all other ethnic groups combined. A major segment of the Tamil community reacted to the Donoughmore Constitution by boycotting the 1931 election to the State Council. The boycott left four northern seats unfilled, further reducing Tamil representation in the first Ceylonese legislature that had any substantial power.[29]

The minorities' anguish over the representation provided by the Donoughmore Constitution and suspicion of revisions being advocated by Sinhalese politicians were expressed in a statement to the secretary

26. For example, see the statement in 1909 by the Jaffna Association, an organization claiming to speak for "the Tamils of the Northern Province, the chief centre of the Tamil population of this Island," in Bandaranaike, *Handbook of the Ceylon National Congress*, pp. 28-32.

27. Donoughmore Report, pp. 92-93; Soulbury Report, pp. 66-67.

28. Donoughmore Report, pp. 101-102. The commission claimed: "The desire to promote the union of the Ceylonese peoples and the conviction that this will only be achieved by the merging of them into a single electorate form indeed the mainspring of our recommendations on this subject." *Ibid.*

29. In 1931, thirty-eight Sinhalese, three Tamils, and five others were elected. Four Tamil constituencies did not return members. In the second State Council election in 1936, thirty-nine Sinhalese, eight Tamils, and three others were elected. See Soulbury Report, pp. 14, 19.

of state for the colonies in 1935 in which the Ceylon Tamil leaders were joined by the Indian Tamils and Muslims of the State Council. The statement deplored the conferral of power on the Sinhalese majority which resulted from the substitution of territorial for communal representation and charged that proposals for constitutional revision were designed to complete Sinhalese domination. The minorities' statement insisted on representation which would prevent the Sinhalese members from outvoting the combined minority representatives in the State Council.[30]

An episode following the second State Council election in 1936 considerably enlarged Tamil apprehension over the transfer of power to a Sinhalese-dominated government and severely tested whatever confidence Tamil leaders may have had in the self-restraint to be expected from a Sinhalese majority in the legislature. Under the unique and experimental executive-committee system created by the Donoughmore Constitution, the State Council members were divided into seven executive committees, each specializing in a broad area of governmental activity and exercising some executive authority. The committee members elected a chairman, called a minister, who sat on a Board of Ministers charged with budgetary responsibilities.[31] Until 1936 the board had included two members of the minority communities. After the 1936 election, the Sinhalese councilors were able to place themselves on committees in such a way that every committee had a Sinhalese majority which chose a Sinhalese as chairman. The result was that the Board of Ministers was composed entirely of Sinhalese. The creation of what was popularly labeled the "pan-Sinhalese ministry" demonstrated the political power implicit in the Sinhalese majority and the capacity and willingness of the Sinhalese legislators to act in concert to the detriment of the minorities.

Sir Baron Jayatilaka, the leader of the State Council, claimed the pan-Sinhalese ministry was prompted by the desire to obtain unanimity on the board for constitutional revision, which was impossible as long as it contained minority ministers. The Colonial Office had cited lack of

30. *Ibid.*, p. 18.
31. On the functioning of the Donoughmore Constitution, see S. Namasivayam, *The Legislatures of Ceylon, 1928-1948* (London: Faber & Faber, Ltd., 1951); I. D. S. Weerawardana, *Government and Politics in Ceylon (1931-1946)* (Colombo: Ceylon Economic Research Association, 1951).

unanimity as a reason for refusal to modify the constitution. Also, the maneuver was designed to demonstrate that the existing constitutional arrangements did not guarantee protection of minority interests.[32] The selection of a Tamil minister in 1942 ended the exclusively Sinhalese ministry. It also ended the unanimity of the board on constitutional revision. In a scheme put forward by the ministers, which considerably influenced the eventual Soulbury Constitution of 1946, the Tamil minister dissented from the proposal for representation.[33]

At about the same time that the pan-Sinhalese ministry was formed, an exclusively and self-consciously Sinhalese political organization appeared. The Sinhala Maha Sabha was organized in the mid-1930's by S. W. R. D. Bandaranaike, a member of the Board of Ministers and a leader of the Ceylon National Congress. Political parties at the time were in an embryonic stage of development. Like other political organizations of the period, when political consciousness was restricted to a small group and ascribed status and personal reputation counted more than program or organization in electoral contests, the Sabha played a minor role in pre-independence politics. The Sabha attracted a number of state councilors, but remained essentially Bandaranaike's personal political vehicle. As party programs and party discipline had not yet crystalized, Bandaranaike simultaneously served as leader of the Sabha and as a member of the executive committee of the Ceylon National Congress. The Sabha had no specific program or clearly defined policies, probably hoping to capitalize on the general sense of Sinhalese communal identification. Bandaranaike denied charges that the Sabha advocated "Ceylon for the Sinhalese."[34] He described the ideas the organization represented as

a very desirable form of communalism, where all that is valuable to a community, its traditions, its culture, its literature, its language is fostered, where an attempt is made to obtain the true advancement of a community by composing the various differences of caste, religion, and so on, within that community, while not forgetting the higher unity, that of communities.[35]

32. Soulbury Report, p. 19.
33. The ministers' scheme appears as Appendix I to the Soulbury Report. The dissent is recorded on p. 121. The Tamil minister was Arunachalam Mahadeva, a son of Sir Ponnambalam Arunachalam.
34. State Council speech of March 21-22, 1939, in S. W. R. D. Bandaranaike, *Towards a New Era* (Colombo: Department of Information, 1961), pp. 50-51.
35. *Ibid.*, p. 67.

The Sabha in fact did not become a source of communal vituperation. Bandaranaike and the Sabha tended to be relatively moderate on issues with communal implications. When the State Council considered the subsequently explosive issue of the official language in 1944, Bandaranaike argued that "it would be ungenerous on our part as Sinhalese not to give due recognition to the Tamil language."[36] The significance of the Sabha lay in the fact that it was a frankly communal organization among the majority Sinhalese. Unlike the Ceylon National Congress, which continued to contain a few members of minority communities and ardently insisted that it was multi-communal, the Sabha was freely described by its leader as having a membership "restricted to Sinhalese."[37] It was an additional sign of the growing role of communal identification in politics.

The Soulbury Commission, charged with recommending further constitutional reform, arrived in Ceylon late in 1944. Shortly before the commission's visit, an organization called the All-Ceylon Tamil Congress was created to present a united defense of Tamil interests in the drafting of the new constitution. The organization, founded by G. G. Ponnambalam, a state councilor from the Jaffna Peninsula, insisted on constitutional and statutory guarantees to protect the minorities against Sinhalese domination after independence. The Tamil Congress took up and championed a plan called by its advocates "balanced representation" and popularly known as the "fifty-fifty" scheme. The scheme, prompted in part by the creation of the pan-Sinhalese ministry, would have limited the Sinhalese to half the seats in the legislature and reserved the remaining half for the minorities. It also would have restricted by statute the members of any one community who could serve in the Cabinet to less than half the Cabinet's membership. Thus, its advocates argued, no community would be in a position to impose its will on the others.[38] The "fifty-fifty" scheme was vigorously urged on the Soulbury Com-

36. Ceylon, State Council, *Debates in the State Council of Ceylon (Hansard)*, 1944, p. 810.

37. Speech at the annual session of the Sinhala Maha Sabha, July 27, 1946, in S. W. R. D. Bandaranaike, *Speeches and Writings* (Colombo: Department of Broadcasting and Information, 1963), p. 114.

38. Soulbury Report, pp. 68-70. Ponnambalam recalled many years later that in the pre-independence debates he "never doubted for a moment" that communal considerations would be of paramount importance in political issues after independence. Interview by the author, July 18, 1965.

mission by Tamil Congress spokesmen, who also charged legislative and administrative discrimination by the Sinhalese State Council majority.

The commission rejected the "fifty-fifty" scheme as a return to communal representation and found no substantial evidence of discrimination against the minorities.[39] However, like the Donoughmore Commission nearly two decades earlier, the Soulbury Commission was apprehensive of the consequences of communalism for Ceylonese politics with the removal of British Imperial control, observing that

> when political issues arise, the populace as a whole tends to divide, not according to the economic and social issues which in the West would ordinarily unite individuals belonging to a particular class, but on communal lines. It is this factor more than any other which makes difficult the application of the principles of Western Democracy to Ceylon.[40]

The commission suggested that the Donoughmore Constitution had been too rigorously majoritarian and indorsed a proposal of the Ceylonese ministers to distribute seats among the nine provinces on the basis of area as well as population, a proposal intended to favor the minorities, who lived in the less heavily populated provinces. The commission also recommended deviation from the principle of equal population in drawing constituency boundaries and the creation of a few multi-member constituencies where these practices would facilitate representation of ethnic or religious minorities.[41] Despite these departures from a strict population basis of representation in order to increase slightly the proportion of parliamentary seats minority members could be expected to win, the commission was unwilling to attempt to negate the Sinhalese numerical predominance. The Tamil and other minorities were given no prospect of avoiding a Sinhalese parliamentary majority.

The constitution resulting from the Soulbury Commission recommendations contained, in addition to the provisions for enhancing the representation of minorities, a limitation on the power of Parliament

39. Soulbury Report, pp. 41-50, 68-69.
40. *Ibid.*, p. 40.
41. *Ibid.*, esp. pp. 70-74. The Delimitation Commission which drew the constituency boundaries for the first election under the Soulbury Constitution concluded that "it would be correct to say that the Soulbury Commission rejected 'a communal basis of election' in favor of a 'territorial basis' but introduced a communal element into their territorial scheme." *Report of the First Delimitation Commission Appointed in Accordance with Sub-section (1) of Section 76 of the Ceylon (Constitution) Order in Council, 1946* (Sessional Paper XIII, 1946), p. 8.

prohibiting the enactment of any law which would impose disabilities or restrictions, or confer advantages or privileges, on members of any community or religion to which members of other communities or religions were not subject.[42] Except for this limitation, which could be overcome by constitutional amendment, the constitution provided for a parliamentary form of government on the British model under a scheme of representation certain to produce a Sinhalese majority.[43]

The Soulbury Constitution, providing for internal autonomy and considered in anticipation of imminent independence, came before the State Council late in 1945. In urging its acceptance, the president of the Ceylon National Congress declared, "On behalf of the Congress and on my own behalf I give the minority communities the sincere assurance that no harm need they fear at our hands in a free Lanka. We want not only a free Lanka. We want a free, united and democratic Lanka."[44] D. S. Senanayake, soon to be the first prime minister under the new constitution, sought to answer "accusations about Sinhalese domination" by citing the constitutional provisions for the protection of minority interests and challenged the Tamils: "Do you want to be governed from London or do you want, as Ceylonese, to help govern Ceylon?"[45] The Tamils apparently accepted the assurances of the Sinhalese leaders. The draft was overwhelmingly approved by the State Council. Only three negative votes were cast, by two Indian Tamils and a Sinhalese.[46] The constitutional issue had been decided in favor of the Sinhalese majority.

The 1947 election, held shortly before independence, was the first Ceylonese election in which political parties played a significant role. The United National party (UNP), formed before the election by most

42. Ceylon (Constitution and Independence) Orders in Council, 1946 and 1947, Article 29, Section 2 (b) and (c).

43. For critical evaluations of the protection subsequently afforded minorities by the constitutional provisions, see S. Namasivayam, *Parliamentary Government in Ceylon, 1948-1958* (Colombo: K. V. G. de Silva & Sons, n.d.), pp. 93-106; and A. J. Wilson, "Minority Safeguards in the Ceylon Constitution," *Ceylon Journal of Historical and Social Studies*, I, 1 (Jan., 1958), 73-95.

44. *Debates in the State Council . . .* , 1945, Vol. II, pp. 6938-6939.

45. The speech is reprinted in S. D. Saparamadu (ed.), *The D. S. Senanayake Memorial Number*, special issue of *Ceylon Historical Journal*, V, 1-4 (July, 1955-April, 1956), 98-106.

46. G. G. Ponnambalam, the Tamil Congress leader, was known to be opposed to the draft but was not present for the vote.

of the prominent politicians of the Ceylon National Congress and the State Council, won the election and formed the first Cabinet with some support from independents. Although led by Low-Country Sinhalese, the UNP contained a few Tamils and contested seats in the Tamil areas. The election was not generally fought on communal issues. Most constituencies were ethnically homogeneous and Sinhalese contested Sinhalese in some areas while Tamil contested Tamil in others. Communal implications could be observed, however, in the fact that with few exceptions the successful candidates everywhere were of the same community as the majority of their constituents. Furthermore, no multicommunal party won a seat in the Tamil North. Seven candidates of the Tamil Congress were elected and most other successful Tamil aspirants were independents. The Sinhalese held about two-thirds of the seats in the new Parliament. Of ninety-five elected members, sixty-eight were Sinhalese and thirteen were Ceylon Tamils. The balance of the elected members consisted of seven Indian Tamils, six Muslims, and one Burgher.[47] The appointment of six members, to represent economic as well as communal interests, added four Europeans and two Burghers.

An indication of the direction majority-minority political relations were to take appeared in the contest for the city of Jaffna seat in the 1947 election. Labeled the "Battle of Jaffna" by the newspapers, the contest produced a direct clash between two prominent Tamil politicians who symbolized the opposing political courses open to the Tamils. G. G. Ponnambalam sought election as a candidate and the founder-leader of the Tamil Congress, an explicitly Tamil political organization. His adversary, Arunachalam Mahadeva, a member of the Board of Ministers, fought as a UNP candidate stressing the need for Tamil political collaboration with the Sinhalese majority. Ponnambalam won an overwhelming victory, collecting nearly three-fourths of the votes cast.[48] The contest was an early and stark illustration of the Tamil voters' preference for political parties exclusively devoted to the Tamil community's interests.

The perennial clashes between Sinhalese and Tamil politicians from 1921 to 1946 can easily lead to exaggeration of the intensity of com-

47. Sir W. Ivor Jennings, "The Ceylon General Election of 1947," *University of Ceylon Review*, VI, 3 (July, 1948), 133-195.
48. Ceylon Daily News, *Parliament of Ceylon, 1947* (Colombo: Associated Newspapers of Ceylon, Ltd., n.d.), pp. 12, 65.

munal conflict in the period. Communal lines were sharply drawn primarily on constitutional questions, carrying implications for future control of the government. Voting in the State Council on the other issues seldom produced a clear division between communities.[49] The rivalry which occurred was strikingly peaceful and orderly. Political awareness had hardly seeped down to the masses by the time of independence, and popular emotionalism was notably absent from the political controversies of the day. The disputation was almost entirely limited to the middle class, which was generally moderate and restrained and, despite ethnic and political differences, was united by class, education, and mode of living.

The growth of communal rivalry was closely connected with the growth of political awareness and activity. Governor Sir Andrew Caldecott, writing in 1938, remarked:

It is said on all sides that sectionalism [i.e., communalism] has increased under the present Constitution; but my observation is that its increase is limited to the political field and has not extended to the every day walks of life where there is a large measure of fellowship and understanding.[50]

Communalism in politics did not arise as a manifestation of acute social antagonisms. Rather, communal competition appeared with the development of the political process and threatened to corrode the tolerant, if not intimate, social relationships which existed between communities. With the increasing responsiveness of the government to Ceylonese opinion, the existing sense of communal identification and loyalty dictated that communal interests and aspirations be protected and promoted in the political sphere. In addition, the benefits and deprivations dependent on political action had multiplied with the rapid expansion of the functions of a modern state. It was, therefore, almost inevitable that growing communal rivalry should accompany the emergence of a modern participant political process in the twentieth century.

49. Namasivayam, *Legislatures of Ceylon*, pp. 60-67. The conclusion that despite political disagreements slight communal tension existed during the two decades preceding independence was reached by two scholars studying the politics of the period, one of whom was a Sinhalese and the other a Tamil. See *ibid.*; and Weerawardana, *Government and Politics in Ceylon*, p. 139 and *passim*.

50. Great Britain, Colonial Office, *Correspondence Relating to the Constitution of Ceylon*, Cmd. 5910 (London: His Majesty's Stationery Office, 1938), p. 8.

CHAPTER II

Sinhalese national resurgence

At about the time of the emergence of the Westernized middle class, which soon began agitation for self-government, a number of religious, social reform, ideological, and literary movements and trends appeared which reflected the growth of a new group self-awareness and self-assertion among the Sinhalese. There was considerable interaction and overlapping of ideas, goals, and personnel among the various movements. The religious and social reform movements preceded and contributed directly to the political movement for self-rule. However, during the twentieth century a divergence became evident between the movement for self-government, which utilized Western language and techniques to seek modern secular goals defined by Western ideology, and the cultural and literary developments, which remained of marginal political importance until after independence and which sought inspiration in the Sinhalese past and rejected the changes induced by Western penetration.

The earliest and probably the strongest force in awakening a Sinhalese national resurgence was a new militant and revivalist spirit among Sinhalese Buddhists. The Theravada Buddhism of the Sinhalese had from very early times played a vital role in cementing Sinhalese self-identification. According to legend, the Sinhalese arrival in Ceylon coincided with the death of the Buddha.[1] For a period of more than a thousand years little is known of Sinhalese history that is not derived from the works of scholarly bhikkhus, who emphasized the close interweaving of the destinies of the Sinhalese people and the Buddhist religion. The concept of Ceylon as the *Dharmadvipa*—the island destined to preserve and propagate the Buddha's doctrine—has been a powerful belief for two millennia.[2] Buddhism had suffered a decline under the

1. As recorded in *The Mahāvaṃsa or the Great Chronicle of Ceylon*, trans. Wilhelm Geiger (London: Oxford University Press, 1912), p. 55.
2. See L. S. Perera, "The Pali Chronicle of Ceylon," in C. H. Philips (ed.), *His-*

Christian, secular, and materialist onslaught of the West. The coming
of Western colonialism cut Buddhism adrift from the patronage of Sinhalese kings, and the crumbling of feudalism further disrupted the
economic and social base of Buddhism and the sangha. Christianity, introduced by the Portuguese in the sixteenth century, was spread for
three centuries through aggressive proselytizing by missionaries with
the support of colonial governments.[3]

Religious and ideological restiveness during the nineteenth century
appeared in an eruption of movements for the purification and rejuvenation of Buddhism and the sangha. At the beginning of the century,
the conservative, Kandyan-dominated Siam Nikāya (sect) was the only
source of ordination for bhikkhus on the island. Resentment by members of the increasingly wealthy and influential Karāva, Salāgama,
and Durāva castes against exclusion from the sangha by the Siam
Nikāya, which restricted ordination to members of the Goyigama caste,
and low-country dissatisfactions resulting from the differences of ethos
and interests separating the changing coast and the more traditional
Kandyan interior led during the century to the formation of several new
sects of bhikkhus through independent ordination in Burma.[4] The last
of these, the Rāmanya Nikāya, was established in 1862 to promote a
tightening of discipline within the sangha and a return to the pure
Theravada doctrine.

A Buddhist revival, which became a popular movement of the laity
as well as the sangha, had generated considerable strength and militancy by the late 1860's. Much of the momentum for the revival was
provided by the low-country castes and classes which had been involved
in the social and economic changes increasingly felt in the coastal areas.[5]

torians of India, Pakistan, and Ceylon (London: Oxford University Press, 1961), pp.
29-43; and E. F. C. Ludowyk, The Footprint of the Buddha (London: George Allen
& Unwin, 1958), pp. 108-110.

3. The impact on Buddhism of nineteenth-century British colonial policy is described in K. M. de Silva, Social Policy and Missionary Organizations in Ceylon, 1840-
1855 (London: Longmans, Green and Co., Ltd., for the Royal Commonwealth Society,
1965), esp. pp. 29-141; and H. D. Evers, "Buddhism and British Colonial Policy in
Ceylon, 1815-1875," Asian Studies, II, 3 (Dec., 1964), 323-333.

4. M. D. Raghavan, The Karāva of Ceylon (Colombo: K. V. G. de Silva & Sons,
1961), pp. 136-138; Bryce Ryan, Caste in Modern Ceylon (New Brunswick, N.J.:
Rutgers University Press, 1953), pp. 39-40.

5. The connection between the social and economic change in the low country and
this revival and later movements for the revitalization of Buddhism is examined in
Michael Ames, "Ideological and Social Change in Ceylon," Human Organization (spe-

Many leaders of the revival were members of the middle-class lay intelligentsia who had been educated in the Christian missionary schools of the Southwest and had reacted to Christian evangelicalism by developing a renewed interest in Buddhism and enthusiasm for its regeneration. Buddhist counterattacks against Christian proselytizing touched off a series of public debates and produced a flurry of polemical pamphlets and newspapers, many in Sinhalese, arguing both the Buddhist and Christian positions. A prominent role in the Buddhist-Christian disputes was assumed by bhikkhus of the sects formed through Burmese ordination earlier in the century. The most famous of the debates, called the Panadura controversy, was held in 1873 and was acclaimed as a great triumph of the eloquent bhikkhu Migettuvatte Gunananda over his Christian adversary.

The publicity produced by the Panadura controversy attracted the American theosophist Colonel Henry Steele Olcott, who arrived in Ceylon in 1880 and immediately embraced Buddhism in a public ceremony at Galle. Olcott played a critical role in the revival of Buddhism and the related awakening of Sinhalese national consciousness by providing the hitherto missing element of organization. The Buddhist Theosophical Society was established as an organization of the Buddhist laity in the year of Olcott's arrival. The society gave the Buddhist revival a new militancy. In an effort to counter the educational activities of Christian missionary groups, the society began to establish Buddhist schools. By 1890, nearly fifty had been opened, one of which later became the prominent Ananda College. Olcott and the society also turned out newspapers and pamphlets and designed a multi-colored Buddhist flag still in wide use among Sinhalese Buddhists. Olcott made a further contribution by helping to develop the ideology of the movement. He gave explicit emphasis to the link between Buddhism and Sinhalese history and extolled the glories of the ancient Sinhalese civilization. By his stress on an idealized Sinhalese past, Olcott helped spur the Buddhist revival in the direction of Sinhalese national resurgence.[6]

A renewal of interest in religious, linguistic, and historical studies

---

cial issue: "Contours of Culture Change in South Asia," ed. William L. Rowe), XXII, 1 (Spring, 1963), 45-53.

6. See D. C. Vijayavardhana, *The Revolt in the Temple* (Colombo: Sinha Publications, 1953), p. 117.

of Ceylon, often pioneered by British civil servants, accompanied the Buddhist revival. Archeological investigations uncovered evidence of the highly developed Sinhalese civilization centered at Anuradhapura and Polonnaruva and helped to open the field of Ceylon antiquity to research. Historical works, Sinhalese and Pali grammars and dictionaries, and translations of Buddhist texts were published. The Ceylon Branch of the Royal Asiatic Society was founded shortly before mid-century. An effort to re-establish the traditional pattern of Buddhist scholarship and learning led to the opening of a number of *pirivenas* modeled on the ancient centers of Buddhist studies. The first of the new *pirivenas* was established in 1839, followed by the founding of the Vidyodaya and Vidyalankara *pirivenas* in the 1870's. Study at the *pirivenas* was concentrated on oriental language and religion.

The Buddhist revival led to and fused with a growth of social welfare and reform movements within the nascent middle class. A temperance movement sprang up at the beginning of the twentieth century and attracted many prominent Ceylonese. The movement was not only related to Buddhist precepts but had discernible anti-colonial overtones. The consumption of intoxicants was seen as an alien habit introduced by Ceylon's European overlords, which contributed through the revenue it produced to the support of the colonial regime. Temperance meetings frequently became platforms for criticism of the government.[7] Presumably because of these anti-colonial and anti-government tendencies, the movement was watched with suspicion by the colonial administration and many of its leaders were jailed during the 1915 riots. Among other reform organizations was the Ceylon Social Reform League, founded by Ananda Coomaraswamy in 1905 to encourage the social improvement of the Ceylonese and discourage the adoption of Western customs.[8] The Ceylon National Association and the Ceylon National Congress obtained most of their early members from the ranks of these social reform movements.

A central role in the crystalization of Sinhalese national self-consciousness out of the religious and social movements and developing reaction to Western cultural and political domination was played by one

7. Kumari Jayawardena, "Birth Centenary of the Anagarika Dharmapala: His Impact on Politics Was Decisive and Far Reaching," *Ceylon Daily News*, Sept. 16, 1964.
8. E. F. C. Ludowyk, *The Story of Ceylon* (London: Faber & Faber, Ltd., 1962), p. 237.

of the most striking figures produced by modern Ceylon, known to the world as Anagarika Dharmapala. Born David Hewavitarane in 1864, a son of a wealthy Colombo entrepreneur of high traditional status, Dharmapala received an English education, passed a public service examination, and became a clerk in the Education Department. He soon abandoned what appeared to be a typical middle-class career, however, to become the most powerful advocate and effective propagandist of resurgent Buddhism. Like many other Buddhist children, Dharmapala had attended a series of Catholic and Anglican schools, where he acquired along with a modern Western education an unrelenting hostility toward Christian proselytizing, which he associated with cultural Westernization and political subjugation. While a young man, he came under the influence of Colonel Olcott and the Russian mystic Helena Petrovna Blavatsky and in 1884 joined the Buddhist Theosophical Society. He resigned his government clerkship and plunged into religious, reform, and welfare activities, assuming the symbolic name of Anagarika (homeless one) Dharmapala (defender of the Buddhist doctrine). He acquired an international reputation as a Buddhist evangelist, attending the World Parliament of Religions in Chicago in 1893 as the representative of Theravada Buddhism and traveling and lecturing extensively in America, Europe, and Japan. Many of his later years were spent in India.[9]

In Dharmapala were combined the Buddhist revivalist, social reformer, and dedicated nationalist. He not only preached the Buddha Dharma, but energetically criticized colonial rule, urged temperance and social regeneration, championed expanded education, and assailed the economic exploitation of Ceylon by foreigners. He encouraged early indications of working-class militancy and hailed Ceylon's first major strike in 1912 as a manifestation of national awakening.[10] He became a severe critic of Western political domination of Ceylon, which he saw as contributing to the moral and material decline of the Sinhalese. His linking of social distress and colonial subjugation was suggested in the notation in his diary: "Poverty, misery, indolence, ignorance every-

9. See Anagarika Dharmapala, *Return to Righteousness*, ed. Ananda Guruge (Colombo: Anagarika Dharmapala Birth Centenary Committee, Ministry of Education and Cultural Affairs, 1965), esp. pp. 697-712; and the Bhikshu Sangharakshita, *Anagarika Dharmapala: A Biographical Sketch* (Kandy: Buddhist Publication Society, 1964).

10. Kumari Jayawardena, "Anagarika Dharmapala and the Early Labour Movement in Ceylon," *Ceylon Daily News*, Sept. 18, 1964.

where. It is a shame this progress under British rule."[11] He once observed: "There is something about alien rule, no matter how beneficent,
that stupefies."[12] Suspicions aroused by Dharmapala's agitation for reform and revival prompted the colonial government to order his in-
ternment in Calcutta and the suppression of his newspaper *Sinhala
Bauddhayā* (*Sinhalese Buddhist*) during the 1915 Buddhist-Muslim
riots.[13]

Dharmapala sought to rekindle a sense of solidarity and self-respect
among the Sinhalese. He described one of his countless speeches thus:
"Spoke to them to be patriotic, that the Sinhalese should be united,
that they were a great and unique people."[14] He extolled the past greatness of the Sinhalese and condemned their modern subservience. He
once wrote in his diary: "Sinhalese must wake up from their slumber.
Blessed island is Ceylon. I will go from town to town declaring the
greatness of our ancestors. . . . We were a great people."[15] Dharmapala
came to symbolize a Sinhalese national resurgence which included ideali-
zation of the Sinhalese past and rejection of Western influences. He
also contributed to the growth of an aggressively tradition-oriented,
anti-Western strand of Sinhalese nationalist sentiment.

Dharmapala and his followers, looking back to ancient Sinhalese
history and traditions for inspiration, condemned the extensive Westernization and alienation from Sinhalese culture of the members of the
middle class. The Western-educated Sinhalese was characterized by
Dharmapala as "a useless entity" who "does nothing for the welfare of
the Sinhalese race,"[16] and by Ananda Coomaraswamy as "sadly de-
generate and de-nationalized."[17] This denunciation of the Westernized
Sinhalese was carried forward by a group of popular writers in the Sinhalese language. A Sinhalese literary renaissance of modest propor-

11. "Diary Leaves of the Late Ven. Anagarika Dharmapala," ed. Sri D. Valisinha,
Maha Bodhi (Calcutta), LXVIII, 12 (Dec., 1960), 384.
12. Dharmapala, *Return to Righteousness*, p. 694.
13. The colonial regime maintained a watch on Dharmapala's activities and several
times considered prosecuting him for sedition. His brother was arrested during the 1915
riots and died in prison. On Dharmapala's relations with the government, see Guruge's
introduction, *ibid.*, pp. liii–lxxiv.
14. "Diary Leaves," *Maha Bodhi*, LXVII, 3–4 (March–April, 1959), 83.
15. *Ibid.*, p. 82.
16. Dharmapala, *Return to Righteousness*, p. 525.
17. Ananda K. Coomaraswamy, *Medieval Sinhalese Art* (Broad Campden, England:
Essex House Press, 1908), p. 15.

tions followed the Buddhist revival and fostered the appearance of Sinhalese-language newspapers, novels, plays, and short stories. Hostility toward Western cultural penetration and contempt for the Sinhalese who abandoned their ancestral culture for Western language, manners, habits, and values were common themes of the new group of writers in Sinhalese.

The most popular of the Sinhalese writers was Piyadasa Sirisena, who had been influenced by Dharmapala and used the then unfamiliar medium of the novel and his newspaper, named *Siṅhala Jātiya* (*Sinhalese Nation*), to call for the religious and cultural regeneration of the Sinhalese through a return to the values of the past. The wholesale condemnation of the English-speaking class for succumbing to Western, modern, and Christian influences gained wide circulation in Sirisena's Sinhalese-language novels at the beginning of the present century. His most popular work, *Jayatissa saha Rosalin hevat Vāsanāvanta Vivāhaya* (*Jayatissa and Rosalin or the Happy Marriage*), was published in 1906. In the following decade, 25,000 copies were sold—a considerable number in view of the small size of the Sinhalese reading public and its unfamiliarity with fiction writing.[18] The exaltation of the Sinhalese past and the attack on Westernization were carried on by other writers. Gramophone records of John de Silva's plays depicting dramatic moments in Sinhalese history or satirizing the adoption of Western habits and manners by the Sinhalese were described by Denham as popular village favorites in the first decade of the century.[19] The writings of Simon de Silva, T. G. W. de Silva, M. C. F. Perera, and Martin Wickremasinghe continued the ridicule and denunciation of the Westernized Sinhalese.

This tradition-oriented nationalist sentiment was primarily concerned with religious and cultural matters and grew separately from the political independence movement shepherded by the Ceylon National Congress. Indeed, the main barbs of the Sinhalese traditionalists were directed at the very Westernized individuals who composed the Congress. Although originating in the same social and ideological discontents and sharing hostility toward colonial rule, the two streams of sentiment

18. E. R. Sarathchandra, *The Sinhalese Novel* (Colombo: M. D. Gunasena & Co., Ltd., 1950), pp. 92-96.

19. E. B. Denham, *Ceylon at the Census of 1911* (Colombo: Government Printer, 1912), p. 173.

developed markedly different characteristics. The Congress was led by
men who, although occasionally displaying a sentimental attachment to
the Sinhalese past and idealized village life, used the English language
for the home and the public platform and adopted Western dress,
manner of living, and mode of thought. Whereas the Sinhalese traditionalists defined their social and cultural goals by reference to the
Sinhalese past, the congressmen tended to seek their goals in a closer
emulation of modern Britain.

The independence movement and the politics revolving around the
State Council continued to be dominated by the Westernized Ceylonese,
who were scarcely aware of the traditionalist onslaught.[20] With independence, the Westernized middle-class politicians came into undisputed
power. The accusations of alienation and abandonment of Sinhalese customs, however, found a small audience among the teachers in the Sinhalese-language village schools and the Sinhalese-educated small
landowners, traders, *ayurvedic* physicians, and other village notables.
Reverberations of the traditionalist accusations gained strength after
independence.[21] A widespread revulsion against the Westernization and
estrangement of the middle class, from which political leadership continued to be drawn, grew closely intertwined with the rise of the official
language issue, eventually swamping the mild, Western-oriented nationalist sentiments preserved by the Congress and later the United
National party.[22]

The influence of this tradition-oriented nationalism appeared in the
hostility toward the Westernized class and rejection of Western influences of a widely circulated post-independence exposition of Sinhalese
national resurgence:

20. The English-educated, middle-class Sinhalese were not entirely free of ambiva-
lence toward their own Westernization and stresses stemming from a sense of alienation
from their ancestral culture. E.g., see Chitra Fernando, "Asian Xenophobia Against
the West," *Annals of the American Academy of Political and Social Science*, CCCXVIII
(July, 1958), 86-87; and Hector Abhayavardhana *et al.*, *The Role of the Western-
Educated Elite*, Community Pamphlet No. 1 (Colombo: Community Institute, 1962),
passim.

21. See E. R. Sarathchandra, "Some Problems Connected with Cultural Revival in
Ceylon," *Bulletin of the Institute of Traditional Cultures, Madras*, 1962, Part I, pp.
1-11.

22. The nationalist attitudes typical of the Congress and UNP are described in Sir
W. Ivor Jennings, *Nationalism and Political Development in Ceylon*, Secretariat Paper
No. 10 (New York: Institute of Pacific Relations, 1950), pp. 11-18.

Since English education and the Christian faith were the keys to lucrative Government jobs, a hybrid class of half-educated, Europeanized Sinhalese was soon formed. Buddhism and the Sinhalese language, Sinhalese customs and manners, and even personal names, came to be looked down upon as the contemptible residues of oriental barbarism. . . . It was the lowest ebb the Sinhalese as a nation had ever reached.[23]

These sentiments were reasserted in a 1965 Independence Day speech by Prime Minister Sirimavo Bandaranaike:

Centuries of colonial rule had cut us adrift from our heritage. For some time after our formal independence, we unfortunately still remained wedded to alien values and guided by alien practices. Western culture, western habits, western education, still occupied the primary place, and our indigenous way of life was relegated to a lower status. The top-hat and the imperial honour became the symbols of our cultural subjugation, although politically we were free. From this state of affairs we have advanced far.[24]

The cultural, social, and political trends emanating from the religious revival were pre-eminently Sinhalese developments. At a number of points parallel developments occurred among the Tamils, or Tamils were involved along with the Sinhalese. The Buddhist revival was accompanied by a revival of smaller dimensions within Hinduism. The Society for the Propagation of Saivism was founded in 1888 by middle-class Tamil Hindus to combat Christian proselytizing and promote Hindu education.[25] The Ramakrishna Mission, founded with the backing of Swami Vivekananda in the next decade, and the closely related Hindu lay organization, the Vivekananda Society, organized in 1902, established Hindu schools and encouraged the rejuvenation of Hinduism.[26] The social and political reform movements included members of the Tamil as well as the Sinhalese elite, but were principally under Sinhalese leadership. Even the reaction to Westernization included among its leading spokesmen Ananda Coomaraswamy, a cousin of the Ponnambalam brothers, who attacked Western education and the consequent alienation of the Western-educated from their own traditions and

23. Vijayavardhana, *The Revolt in the Temple*, p. 116.
24. "Prime Minister's Independence Day Message," *Ceylon Today*, XIV, 2 (Feb., 1965), 6.
25. G. C. Mendis, *Ceylon Under the British* (2nd ed. rev.; Colombo: Colombo Apothecaries Co., Ltd., 1948), p. 90.
26. James Cartman, *Hinduism in Ceylon* (Colombo: M. D. Gunasena & Co., Ltd., 1957), pp. 179-182.

culture.[27] Coomaraswamy, however, was primarily criticizing the Sinhalese, among whom the process of Westernization had gone much farther than among the more conservative Tamils.

Generally, Tamil society seemed less touched by the manifestations of social and political restiveness. In part, this was no doubt a reflection of the fact that the Tamils were a minority, and events in the Sinhalese community assumed much greater magnitude. In addition, however, the nineteenth-century economic and social changes were most strongly felt in the Sinhalese areas of the Southwest and Tamil society apparently suffered a less rapid or drastic dislocation. Although Tamils took readily to Western education, the Western-educated Tamils usually went to the South for employment, and the impact of their Westernization on Tamil society in the North was lessened. Even the Western-educated Tamils seem to have less readily or less completely abandoned their traditional culture for an almost totally Western way of life. As Tamil social organization was more rigid and tightly woven than Sinhalese, it appears to have offered greater resistance to the impact of Western culture.[28]

The kindling of Sinhalese self-awareness was not necessarily antagonistic toward the Tamils and other minorities. The Buddhist revivalists commonly viewed Hinduism as a sister Eastern religion, also suffering from the oppression of Western Christians. The elements in the Sinhalese awakening, however, tended to emphasize Sinhalese uniqueness to the exclusion of other communities and to encourage the growth of group solidarity among the Sinhalese. The revival of Buddhism strengthened realization of the unique bonds between Buddhism and the Sinhalese. When memories of the past were recalled, it was a Sinhalese past which was remembered. Revived memories of the ancient wars between Sin-

27. E.g., Coomaraswamy, *Medieval Sinhalese Art*, pp. 15-17, 51, 255. Unlike many of the traditionalists, Coomaraswamy was not parochial in his background or attitudes. He was educated in Britain, his mother was British, and he spent a considerable part of his career with the Museum of Fine Arts in Boston. He was best known for his sweeping interpretations of the art and philosophy of the Indian cultural area.

28. See Elsie K. Cook, *Ceylon: Its Geography, Its Resources and Its People*, rev. K. Kularatnam (2nd ed.; Madras: Macmillan and Company, Ltd., 1951), pp. 245-247. On Sinhalese social organization, see Bryce Ryan, L. D. Jayasena, and D. C. R. Wickremesinghe, "Secularization Processes in a Ceylon Village," *Eastern Anthropologist*, XI, 3-4 (March-Aug., 1958), 155-161; and Murray A. Straus, "Childhood Experience and Emotional Security in the Context of Sinhalese Social Organization," *Social Forces*, XXXIII, 2 (Dec., 1954), 152-160.

halese and Tamils, preserved in the *Mahāvaṃsa* and the folk-legends of the Sinhalese, emphasized the past periods of struggle with Tamil invaders and tended to depict the Sinhalese people's triumphs and humiliations as victories or defeats in contests with the Tamils. Eventually, the Sinhalese national resurgence tended to lead from an emphasis on the uniqueness of the Sinhalese to an insistence on obtaining for the Sinhalese community the position and prerogatives of the majority, ultimately contributing to the power of the movement for Sinhalese as the sole official language.

CHAPTER III

Origin of the language issue

The official language issue emerged shortly after independence as the most explosive and divisive issue of Ceylonese politics, frequently overshadowing and submerging the innumerable other questions of public policy facing the island. The situation in which the official language could become the center of bitter controversy was a consequence of Western colonial rule, which left Ceylon at independence with a government geared throughout to function in the English language, a small group of Ceylonese educated in English, and a large and growing population literate in Sinhalese and Tamil. Although under the encouragement of the Portuguese rulers in the sixteenth and seventeenth centuries the Portuguese language acquired some importance in the coastal towns, a European language did not penetrate significantly into Ceylon until the nineteenth century. The Portuguese and Dutch employed their own languages for record-keeping and some central government purposes, but exercised authority over the Ceylonese population in the languages of the island. Both powers relied for the most part on indirect rule through the indigenous aristocracy and were unable to extend their authority beyond the coastal areas. The language of government became a crucial question in the period of British rule both because the British Imperial policy regarding language differed and because after the late nineteenth century the state became of much greater importance to the Ceylonese.

Language, education, and opportunity

From the commencement of British rule at the end of the eighteenth century, Ceylon was in practice governed in English. Beginning early in the nineteenth century, English education was provided on a limited scale in order to train Ceylonese to staff the clerical and lower grades of the public service. English was employed for the records, directives, and reports produced by the Colombo secretariat and the provincial government offices, the *kachcheris*. The far-ranging reports of Lieutenant-Colonel W. M. G. Colebrooke and C. H. Cameron in 1831-1832 provided a major impetus to the use of English in administration, the courts, and the schools. Colebrooke called for the opening of greater opportunities in the public service to Ceylonese, but stressed the necessity for recruits to possess competence in English. He also urged more vigorous efforts in the field of English education.[1] The Colebrooke-Cameron proposals preceded by a few years Thomas Macaulay's famous "Minute on Education" in India, written in 1835, and reflected a similar attitude toward the civilizing role of European language and learning in Asia. Following Colebrooke's recommendations, the government abandoned its small number of Sinhalese and Tamil schools and opened five English schools in the major cities. Within a few years an English secondary school was established by the government in Colombo to train teachers. By 1848, the number of government schools providing education in English had risen to sixty.[2]

Knowledge of English was essential for employment in the expanding public service. Through the nineteenth century, the number of Ceylonese employed in the colonial bureaucracy grew steadily. By 1868, more than 80 per cent of the 1,084 public service appointments, including 92 of the 282 posts in the higher grades, were held by Ceylonese.[3] In 1875, Ponnambalam Arunachalam became the first Ceylonese to enter the small and select Ceylon Civil Service by competitive examination. The predominance of Europeans in the staff and professional grades of the public service gradually declined as increasing numbers of Ceylonese trained in English acquired higher educations, first at British universities and later at professional schools and a university college on the island.

1. See G. C. Mendis (ed.), *The Colebrooke-Cameron Papers: Documents on British Colonial Policy in Ceylon, 1796-1833* (London: Oxford University Press, 1956), I, 70-75. For an account of British Imperial policy regarding the language of government and education in Asia and its social and political consequences, see Hugh Tinker, "People and Government in Southern Asia," in *Transactions of the Royal Historical Society*, Ser. 5, Vol. IX (London: Royal Historical Society, 1959), pp. 141-167.

2. G. C. Mendis, *Ceylon Under the British* (2nd ed. rev.; Colombo: Colombo Apothecaries Co., Ltd., 1948), p. 53.

3. Lennox A. Mills, *Ceylon Under British Rule, 1795-1932* (London: Oxford University Press, 1933), pp. 91-92.

The commanding position of English extended beyond the public service to the professions and private commercial and financial establishments. All the remunerative and prestigious careers were open only to those with a knowledge of English. A state councilor once explained the attitude toward language prevalent in the early decades of the twentieth century:

My father was a great Sinhalese scholar. . . . [B]ut he never sent me to a Sinhalese school or taught me Sinhalese. It was simply because he felt that English was the official language of the country, and for material gain and benefit the only language that counted was the English language. I am sure many parents in this country felt in the same way.[4]

The demand for English education mounted rapidly. Ceylonese who advanced economically through trade, crafts, or agriculture avidly sought to educate their children in English. The connection between education and social mobility was ably described by E. B. Denham in his report on Ceylon in 1911:

The older generation regard education as an investment for their children, which will enable them to take up positions to which their newly-acquired wealth entitles them. The small landowner and cultivator who has prospered believes that education will make a clerk of his son or fit him for a learned profession, that the latter will then hold a better position in the world than his father, and that consequently the fortunes and, what appeals to him equally strongly, the status of the family will be assured. The younger generation seek escape from rural life, from manual toil, from work which they begin to regard as degrading, in an education which will enable them to pass examinations, which will lead to posts in offices in the towns, and so to appointments which entitle the holders to the respect of the class from which they believe they have emancipated themselves.

Denham added: "The demand has passed considerably beyond the desire for a good vernacular education, which is no longer associated with advancement; it is now a popular clamour for an English education."[5] Enrolment in government and state-assisted English schools climbed from approximately 7,000 in 1880 to nearly 21,000 in 1900, to 37,000 in 1920. By 1945 the figure had passed 100,000.[6]

4. Ceylon, State Council, *Debates in the State Council of Ceylon (Hansard)*, 1944, p. 761.
5. E. B. Denham, *Ceylon at the Census of 1911* (Colombo: Government Printer, 1912), p. 399.
6. For the period 1880-1911, *Report of the Director of Public Instruction* (Colombo:

The provision of education in English, however, seldom kept pace with the growing demand. Education in a tongue foreign to more than 90 per cent of the population presented almost insuperable difficulties, which were increasingly realized in the latter decades of the nineteenth century. The idea that the government bore a responsibility for the general diffusion of education among the population had begun to take root in the Colonial Office and the government of Ceylon. As the objective shifted from the production of a limited number of government clerks to the education of the vast masses of the island, the prospect of attempting education in a language unknown to the overwhelming majority of the potential students led to a new outlook on education in the "vernacular"—the term invariably used for Sinhalese and Tamil. The quality and results of education in English had been a source of frequent disappointment and a subject of repeated criticism. The belief developed that considerably greater success could be achieved by education commenced, at least, in the language of the home. The optimism and enthusiasm for English which had characterized Colebrooke, Cameron, and Macaulay gradually receded. In about 1885, the government shifted to an emphasis on vernacular education, largely abandoning the field of English education to the Christian missionaries.[7] This was followed by a tremendous expansion in literacy and the number of schools and school-going children.

Mass education in Ceylon has been synonymous with vernacular education. After the 1880's, more than 80 per cent of the student enrolment each year was in vernacular schools. In 1880, 42,475 students were enrolled in government and assisted vernacular schools. The number soared to 148,181 in 1900, 322,177 in 1920, and 690,600 in 1945.[8] By 1953, 65 per cent of the population five years of age and over was literate, compared with 17 per cent in 1881.[9] Literacy in 1953 was overwhelmingly in the individual's "mother tongue," which for about 98

Government Printer, 1881-1912); for 1912-1930, *Report of the Director of Education* (Colombo: Government Printer, 1913-1931); and after 1935, *Administration Report of the Director of Education* (Colombo: Government Press, 1936-1946), for the years indicated.

7. See H. A. Wyndham, *Native Education* (London: Oxford University Press, 1933), esp. pp. 47-50.

8. See n. 6 above.

9. Ceylon, Department of Census and Statistics, *Ceylon Year Book, 1958* (Colombo: Government Press, 1959), p. 33.

Table 5. *Literacy in "mother tongue" of Ceylon population five years of age and over, 1953*[a]

Community/ language group	Number five years of age and over	Literate in mother tongue[b]		Not literate in mother tongue, but literate in other language		Illiterate	
		Number	Per cent	Number	Per cent	Number	Per cent
Sinhalese	4,765,970	3,246,447	68.1	37,998	0.8	1,481,525	31.
Tamils[c]	1,593,462	875,174	54.9	26,873	1.7	691,415	43.
Moors	432,861	227,284[d]	52.5	16,572	3.8	189,005	43.
Burghers, Eurasians	39,896	29,600[e]	74.2	5,939	14.9	4,357	10.
Malays	21,290	4,356[f]	20.5	10,046	47.2	6,888	32.
Others[g]	35,587	16,934	47.6	11,574	32.5	7,079	19.

[a]Literacy was defined as "the ability to write a short letter and read the reply to it." Mother tongue was defined as "the language of the race [community] to which the father belonged." Consequently, the Sinhalese language was considered the mother tongue for 69 per cent of the population five years of age and over, and the Tamil language was considered the mother tongue for the Tamils who constituted 23 per cent as well as the Moors who constituted 6 per cent.

[b]Does not exclude literacy in another language in addition to the mother tongue.

[c]Presumably because the Ceylon and Indian Tamils possess the same mother tongue, they are not differentiated in this table of the census report.

[d]Includes 226,111 literate in Tamil and 1,173 literate in Arabic.

[e]Indicates literacy in English.

[f]Includes 4,216 literate in Malay and 140 literate in Arabic.

[g]Consists of Europeans (5,864), Veddahs (632), and "other population" (29,091).

Source: Ceylon, Department of Census and Statistics, *Census of Ceylon, 1953*, Vol. III, Part (Colombo: Government Press, 1960), pp. 5-20, Table 20.

per cent of the population was Sinhalese or Tamil (see Table 5). After nearly a century and a half of education in English, in 1953 English literates constituted only one-seventh of all literate Ceylonese.[10]

The dual system of education differentiated by language had profound social consequences for the island. The division between the English-educated and the vernacular-educated marked a formidable class

10. In 1953, 648,331 Ceylonese were literate in English from a total literate population of 4,508,797. Ceylon, Department of Census and Statistics, *Census of Ceylon, 1953*, I (Colombo: Government Press, 1957), 192, 196. The situation in Ceylon produced by the mobilization of the vast vernacular-speaking population at a more rapid rate than their assimilation to English is comparable to that in India analysed by Karl W. Deutsch, *Nationalism and Social Communication* (Cambridge, Mass.: M.I.T. Press, 1953), pp. 108-111, 197-204. The remarkable extent to which knowledge of English was diffused in Ceylon should not be overlooked, however. The number of Ceylonese literate in English constituted 9.4 per cent of the total population five years of age and over. Nearly one in every eight males five years of age and over (450,354 of 3,659,710) was literate in English in 1953.

barrier. The English-educated held the positions of wealth, prestige, and power. Vernacular education was provided for the cultivators, laborers, village traders, and service workers who formed the broad "masses" of Ceylon. At first limited to elementary training, vernacular schools eventually were extended to the secondary level. However, students leaving the vernacular schools found few desirable occupational opportunities open to them. They were barred from the government service, the island's principal employer of clerks and office workers, and from university or professional training, which required education in English. The Sinhalese- or Tamil-educated students were prepared for few careers more rewarding than that of a teacher in the vernacular village school.[11] Added to the stark contrast in wealth and status was a vast cultural gulf. The English-educated generally abandoned indigenous culture and assumed essentially Western modes of living, while the rest of the society remained much closer to traditional patterns of attitudes and behavior.[12]

Access to the ardently desired English education was highly unequal. While a vernacular education in the village school was free, English schools levied fees which the general population could seldom afford. The best English educations usually necessitated living away from home at expensive boarding schools. Consequently, the opportunity to acquire education in English was linked to wealth and class. English schools were concentrated in the Southwest around Colombo and on the Jaffna Peninsula. The resulting regional inequality of educational opportunity was reflected in enrolments in the University of Ceylon, the vast majority of whose students came from three of Ceylon's nine provinces, the Western, Southern, and Northern.[13] Similarly, most English schools were in the few major cities, more accessible to the small urban than the vast rural population.

With the adoption of universal suffrage and the passage of political

11. See G. C. Mendis, "Adult Franchise and Educational Reform," *University of Ceylon Review*, II, 1-2 (Oct., 1944), 37-44.

12. On the class and cultural divisions produced by English and vernacular education, see H. A. Passé, "The English Language in Ceylon," *ibid.*, I, 2 (Nov., 1943), 50-65; Bryce Ryan, "Status, Achievement and Education in Ceylon," *Journal of Asian Studies*, XX, 4 (Aug., 1961), 471-476; and Ralph Pieris, "Bilingualism and Cultural Marginality," *British Journal of Sociology*, II, 4 (Dec., 1951), 328-339.

13. Sir W. Ivor Jennings, "Race, Religion and Economic Opportunity in the University of Ceylon," *University of Ceylon Review*, II, 1-2 (Oct., 1944), 4.

control to Ceylonese hands, the wide chasm between education in the vernacular village schools and education in the urban English schools came under growing attack. Popular demand for more schools and greater equality of educational opportunity found increasing political expression in the period of the Donoughmore Constitution. Attempts to bridge the gap between English and vernacular education were made, but without conspicuous success. Following the recommendation of a State Council committee in 1943, a decision was made to require that primary education be in the "mother tongue" of the student, with English introduced at a later stage.[14] One attempt to equalize opportunity, while providing mass vernacular education without disturbing the dominant position of English, was recorded by the Soulbury Commission shortly before independence:

The Minister [for Education] aims at the appointment of teachers of English in the Vernacular schools and the establishment of Central schools to which selected pupils may pass for continued education. By this means, children of promise from the villages would have an opportunity of entering into the range of occupations in which a knowledge of English is essential. But so far little progress has been made, largely because of the expense involved.[15]

The language problem as a major political issue almost inexorably followed the creation of a large vernacular-educated electorate. Virtually all positions of honor and remuneration were monopolized by the English-educated. Whether in the public service, the legal profession, or education, most of these careers were linked directly or indirectly with the government and the official language. After the introduction of mass education, more than 80 per cent of the Ceylonese attending school were being educated in the vernacular. English education had not been diffused widely enough to satisfy the rapidly rising demand, producing a gap between aspirations and the capacity for their satisfaction. Although the masses were slow to perceive the power placed in their hands by the introduction of universal suffrage in 1931, the stage was set for a challenge to the dominant position of the English language and the English-educated class.

14. See Wallace R. Muelder, *Schools for a New Nation* (Colombo: K. V. G. de Silva & Sons, 1962), pp. 61-80; J. E. Jayasuriya, "Current Educational Trends and Controversies in Ceylon," *International Review of Education*, VIII, 3-4 (1963), 292-299.
15. Soulbury Report, p. 35.

The swabhasha movement

Gradually a demand for "swabhasha"[16] or the people's "own language" as the language of government and, consequently, the language of social and economic opportunity began to gather strength. The swabhasha movement reflected the frustrations of the vernacular-speaking Ceylonese governed in a language they did not understand and the protest of the vernacular-educated over the social, economic, and political inequalities resulting from the linguistic and educational bifurcation of society.

With English as the language of administration, the people unacquainted with English increasingly found themselves brought into contact with a government functioning in an alien tongue. It is probable that for some time the village cultivator was unconcerned with the language employed in the distant *kachcheri* or Colombo secretariat. The village headman continued to deal with those under his authority in the language of the village. However, as government became more centralized and more active, and as Ceylonese society changed, the awareness and inconvenience of the language gap increased. Licenses, permits, and applications commonly had to be completed in English. Petitions and appeals to the government either had to be in English or were believed to stand a greater chance of favorable response if drafted in English. A Ceylonese making a complaint to the police had his statement recorded in English, which he was required to sign—with slight assurance that it was faithfully reproduced—before action would be taken. Court proceedings were conducted in English, probably to the frequent bewilderment of Sinhalese- or Tamil-speaking defendants undergoing trial in an incomprehensible language.[17] The conduct of government in a language understood by only a small minority of the people produced the phenomenon of the petition-writer, who by virtue

16. According to the system of transliteration used in this work, this word should appear as *svabhāṣā*. However, the expression has been employed in South Asia so frequently in English as "swabhasha" (or "swabhasa") that it appeared desirable to follow this practice here.

17. A poignant scene in a novel written by a British former member of the Ceylon Civil Service vividly describes the fear and incomprehension of a Sinhalese-speaking villager being tried in a court conducting its proceedings in English. See Leonard Woolf, *The Village in the Jungle* (London: Chatto & Windus, 1951), pp. 187-211.

of his esoteric command of the language of government became an essential but not necessarily reliable intermediary between the government and the people. The first rumblings of discontent over the language of government concerned these disadvantages, small and large, faced by the majority of the Ceylonese who did not know English. One of the early attacks on the place of English was the demand by the nascent Marxist Lanka Sama Samaja party in 1936 that proceedings of the lower courts and entries in police records be allowed in the indigenous languages.[18]

Concern over the social and political implications of the language situation and the illogic of operating a democratic government responsible to the people in a language alien to the vast majority of them was frequently expressed in the agitation for the replacement of English. A select committee of the State Council, reporting on the official language in 1946, described the situation prevailing in Ceylon as "a Government of the Sinhalese- or Tamil-speaking 6,200,000, by the English-speaking 20,000 Government servants, for the 400,000 English-speaking public."[19] Earlier, J. R. Jayewardene had reminded the State Council of the great imbalance in the numbers educated in English and in Sinhalese and Tamil and declared:

But the official language is English, and that is why this country is always in danger of being governed by a small coterie who go through those English schools, whereas the vast majority who go through the Sinhalese and Tamil schools must always be in the position of hewers of wood and drawers of water.[20]

Two decades later, describing in retrospect the goals of the swabhasha movement, Prime Minister Sirimavo Bandaranaike emphasized the desire to incorporate the broad masses of the people into the effective life of the polity:

We have tried to eliminate the wide gap which existed between the Government and the governed, between the elite and the masses. . . . By giving the due and rightful place to the Sinhala language as the Official Language of the country, we have made it possible for those voiceless millions who spoke

18. Leslie Goonewardene, *A Short History of the Lanka Sama Samaja Party* (Colombo: Lanka Sama Samaja Party, 1960), pp. 6-7.
19. *Sinhalese and Tamil as Official Languages* (Sessional Paper XXII, 1946), p. 10.
20. *Debates in the State Council . . .* , 1944, p. 747.

only that language, to play an effective part in the affairs of the country. As long as English reigned, their freedom was limited.[21]

Closely associated with these sentiments were demands for equality of opportunity, particularly in public service appointments. The utmost importance has been attached to government employment in Ceylon. The bureaucracy has few rivals in the career preferences of Ceylonese. The high status and prestige enjoyed by the government official may be in part a legacy of the traditional society, in which political office was an attribute of high social position, and great value was placed on titles and symbols of rank. Also, the agricultural economy of Ceylon has offered few attractive alternatives, particularly for the educated person seeking white-collar employment. Expanding education and improved communications heightened awareness of the rewards of status and material gain obtainable through non-agricultural employment. With rising aspirations since the late nineteenth century, a common avenue of social mobility had been education in English and passage of a public service examination, which led to the security, prestige, and relative comfort of a bureaucratic career and eligibility for a sizable dowry.

Those who were unable to obtain English educations for themselves or their children saw the use of English in government as a block to their aspirations and the swabhasha movement as an instrument for breaking the hold of the small English-educated segment of society on government employment. The desire of the vernacular-educated for access to public service employment was reflected in S. W. R. D. Bandaranaike's demand for the swift replacement of English as the official language, which he claimed

is important for this reason . . . if for no other, that over ninety per cent. of the [government] jobs of this country are restricted to ten per cent. of the people who know English. In this land of ours, those ignorant of English are capable of obtaining much less than 10 per cent. of Government jobs![22]

His widow, Sirimavo Bandaranaike, later asked: "Was not the whole idea of independence incomplete so long as an exclusive knowledge of

21. "Sixteenth Anniversary of Independence," *Ceylon Today*, XIII, 2 (Feb., 1964), 6.

22. Speech of September 1, 1953, in S. W. R. D. Bandaranaike, *Towards a New Era* (Colombo: Department of Information, 1961), p. 927.

the English language was more or less the only passport to the Public Service?"[23]

Social injustice stemming from inequalities of educational opportunity and access to public service employment was stressed in a recent look back to the rise of the swabhasha movement. A member of Parliament who was formerly a Sinhalese-language schoolteacher, writing in a political party publication, argued that the English schools, because they were fee-levying, benefited only the children of the aristocratic and wealthy classes. Children of lesser classes had access only to vernacular schools. With English as the official language, the English-educated sons of the privileged classes monopolized the top positions in government, enjoying large salaries and living abundantly, while the vernacular-educated were condemned to unemployment or work as laborers. Thus, English as the official language perpetuated and accentuated a condition of invidious social privilege.[24]

The swabhasha movement drew strength from the earlier Sinhalese national resurgence, which had stimulated sentimental attachment to the Sinhalese language as a part of the Sinhalese cultural heritage and a distinguishing attribute of the national group. The Sinhalese language and Theravada Buddhism were identified as the major factors responsible for preserving the separate existence of the Sinhalese people, differentiating them from the nearby Dravidian-speaking peoples of South India for more than two millennia.[25] "It is because of our language that the Sinhalese race has existed for 2,400 years," the State Council was told in 1944.[26]

Among those concerned for the status or even the survival of the Sinhalese language, the notion developed that the salvation of the language lay in its recognition as the official language of government. If the tremendous weight of vocational advantage in the public service could be placed behind study in Sinhalese, rather than English, and if the

23. *Sunday Times of Ceylon*, Dec. 3, 1961.
24. P. B. Balasuriya, "Bhāṣāvē Nāṅgīma Jātiyē Nāṅgīmayi [The Elevation of the Language Is the Elevation of the Nation]," *Śrī Laṅkā Nidahas Pakṣayē Saṅvatsara Kalāpaya, 1964 [Sri Lanka Freedom Party's Annual Number, 1964]* (Colombo: Sri Lanka Freedom Party, 1964), pp. 57-60.
25. This is the conclusion of the prominent Ceylonese historian, G. C. Mendis. See his *Ceylon Today and Yesterday* (2nd ed. rev.; Colombo: Associated Newspapers of Ceylon, Ltd., 1963), pp. 42-48.
26. *Debates in the State Council . . .* , 1944, p. 748.

prestige of being the official language could enhance the status of education in and use of Sinhalese, the decline of Sinhalese would be halted
and the continued existence of the language would be assured. To the
Sinhalese champions of swabhasha, the very existence of the Sinhalese
people as a unique and distinguishable group was dependent on the
survival of the Sinhalese language, which in turn was dependent on making Sinhalese the official language.

On May 24, 1944, J. R. Jayewardene moved a resolution in the
State Council to make "Sinhalese the official language of Ceylon within
a reasonable number of years." At the behest of Tamil state councilors,
the resolution was amended to provide for both Sinhalese and Tamil as
the official languages. The resolution specified that Sinhalese and Tamil
were to become the languages of instruction in the schools, examinations
for the public service, and proceedings of the legislature. In this form
the resolution was approved by a vote of twenty-seven to two.[27] The
following year the State Council accepted a motion by S. W. R. D.
Bandaranaike to appoint a select committee to study steps necessary to
carry out the change in official languages.[28] The committee, under the
chairmanship of J. R. Jayewardene, in its report issued in 1946 made
a strong appeal for swabhasha, citing the disabilities to which the vernacular-educated and the vernacular languages, particularly Sinhalese,
were subject. The committee recommended a ten-year transition period,
at the end of which English would cease to be the language of government.[29] The committee's report concluded:

We trust that our efforts will remove the gulf that now divides the people
into two classes, and thus not only afford the vast majority of our countrymen
better opportunities of participating fully in the life of the nation, but also
create a cultural and literary renaissance equalling the golden ages of Lanka's
historic past.[30]

At independence in 1948, the political leadership of Ceylon was committed to the gradual transition to Sinhalese and Tamil as official languages. The post-independence United National party Government was
essentially a continuation of the State Council leadership. D. S. Senana-

27. *Ibid.*, 1944, pp. 745-746, 816-817.
28. *Ibid.*, 1945, Vol. II, pp. 6574-6575.
29. *Sinhalese and Tamil as Official Languages*, p. 12.
30. *Ibid.*, p. 48.

yake, formerly leader of the State Council, became prime minister. The Cabinet included Dudley Senanayake, J. R. Jayewardene, and S. W. R. D. Bandaranaike, all of whom had been prominently associated with the swabhasha policy. An Official Languages Commission was created in 1951 and labored until late 1953 at the task of determining the procedure to be followed in adopting Sinhalese and Tamil as official languages.[31] In 1952, D. S. Senanayake died and was succeeded as prime minister by his son, Dudley Senanayake. In an election campaign later in the year, swabhasha received the indorsement of all the major parties although it did not become the predominant campaign issue.[32] Shortly after the election, which produced a solid UNP triumph, Dudley Senanayake stressed to an annual UNP conference both the continued commitment to swabhasha and the necessity for gradualism:

We stated [in the election campaign] that our previous Government . . . had already accepted the principle that these two languages [Sinhalese and Tamil] would be the official languages of Ceylon and that, within a reasonable period of time, the process was to be completed. Steps were to be taken gradually, realizing the practical impossibility of the 24-hour or the one-minute solution.[33]

Despite the reiterated commitment to swabhasha, however, implementation lagged and innumerable reasons for delay were discovered. In its first report, the Official Languages Commission stressed the contrast with the situation in Burma, where the commission claimed a rapid displacement of English as the language of government had been possible because Burmese was still in use even among the English-educated, "whereas Sinhalese has for more than a century been almost a dead language to most of the English-educated Sinhalese."[34] Suspicions developed that the UNP Government's enthusiasm for a rapid shift from English to Sinhalese and Tamil had waned, particularly after Dudley Senanayake resigned as prime minister and was succeeded by his cousin, Sir John Kotelawala, in 1953.

S. W. R. D. Bandaranaike assumed a leading role in the agitation

31. *Final Report of the Official Languages Commission* (Sessional Paper XXII, 1953).

32. I. D. S. Weerawardana, "The General Elections in Ceylon, 1952," *Ceylon Historical Journal*, II, 1-2, (July-Oct., 1952), 111-178.

33. *U.N.P. Journal*, Feb. 13, 1953.

34. *First Interim Report of the Official Languages Commission* (Sessional Paper XXI, 1951), p. 4.

for the immediate adoption of swabhasha. On the formation of the UNP in 1947, Bandaranaike's Sinhala Maha Sabha had entered the new party in a body and Bandaranaike had become a Cabinet minister and UNP officer. The Sabha, however, maintained its separate identity within the UNP.[35] From inside the Government, Bandaranaike began to champion the swabhasha cause, urging on the UNP the need for swift action. In 1951, he resigned from the Cabinet and the Sabha withdrew from the UNP. Bandaranaike is thought to have decided to resign after a struggle for succession to UNP leadership led him to conclude that his hope of succeeding D. S. Senanayake as party leader had been frustrated. The immediate cause of the break was a Sabha resolution charging the UNP Government with procrastination and delay on the language question.[36] Within a few days of his resignation, Bandaranaike launched an attack on the Government for inaction on the official language change and failure to establish a date by which the change was to be effected, claiming to see "no difficulty in the way of the early adoption of our languages."[37] Immediately after his departure from the UNP, Bandaranaike disbanded the Sabha and founded the Sri Lanka Freedom party (SLFP). The newly organized party quickly sought to harness the forces underlying the swabhasha movement, declaring in its first manifesto: "It is most essential that Sinhalese and Tamil be adopted as official languages immediately so that the people of this country may cease to be aliens in their own land; so that an end may be put to the iniquity of condemning those educated in Sinhalese and Tamil to occupy the lowliest walks of life."[38]

The swabhasha movement originated as a protest against the privileges maintained by the small and exclusive English-educated elite and the dearth of opportunities available to the vernacular-educated. It was essentially a class rather than a communal issue until its character began to change in the early 1950's. The extent to which the official language issue was considered a revolt against the place of English rather

35. The Sabha joined the UNP under a provision of the UNP constitution which allowed members of previously existing political organizations to join the party while retaining their earlier organization. See *United National Party Constitution*, rev. Sept. 11, 1948 (Colombo: United National Party, 1948), p. 2.
36. *U.N.P. Journal*, June 29, 1951, and July 20, 1951.
37. Bandaranaike, *Towards a New Era*, pp. 691-693.
38. As quoted in Ceylon, Senate, *Parliamentary Debates (Hansard)*, Vol. 10, col. 593.

than a contest between communities is attested by the ease with which the overwhelmingly Sinhalese State Council accepted the demand for the inclusion of Tamil in the 1944 resolution.

The swabhasha movement was largely a Sinhalese movement. The Tamils had less to gain by securing a change in the official language. The establishment of Christian missionary schools in the North had made English education available very early, and Tamils had taken advantage of the opportunity in substantial numbers. An American Congregationalist mission began educational activities in Jaffna in the second decade of the nineteenth century, founding the English-language school which eventually became Jaffna College. In the early part of the century, the school was credited with being one of the few sources of good English education on the island.[39] Jaffna College gave instruction through the secondary level and eventually prepared students for external London University baccalaureate degrees. Most graduates of the college sought public service careers.[40] The early and relatively abundant provision of English education in the North made it possible for a substantial number of Tamil youths to gain admission to the professions and the clerical and administrative grades of the public service.[41] From the establishment of the University of Ceylon in 1942 until 1960, Tamils constituted more than 30 per cent of the university's students, while Sinhalese formed about 60 per cent.[42] The Tamils had established

39. In 1831, Colonel Colebrooke praised the educational efforts of the American missionaries in Jaffna, who he claimed, unlike the English missionaries, appreciated the importance of providing the Ceylonese with education in English. Mendis, *Colebrooke-Cameron Papers*, I, 73-74.

40. Wyndham, *Native Education*, pp. 44-45; Muelder, *Schools for a New Nation*, pp. 186-190.

41. In a 1921 memorial to the governor, the Tamil Maha Jana Sabha claimed: "In most of the Departments of Government and in the learned professions the number of Sinhalese and Tamils is almost equal. Graduates and Under-graduates of Universities are found among the Tamils in much larger proportion than among any other Ceylonese community." Great Britain, Colonial Office, *Correspondence Relating to the Further Revision of the Constitution of Ceylon*, Cmd. 1809 (London: His Majesty's Stationery Office, 1923), p. 19.

42. Although Ceylon and Indian Tamils are not differentiated in the enrolment figures, very few Indian Tamils have attended the university and the Tamils enrolled are with little doubt almost entirely Ceylon Tamils. See Jennings, "Race, Religion and Economic Opportunity in the University of Ceylon," p. 2. The relative proportion of Sinhalese and Tamils at the university changed little until a rapid expansion of enrolment coincided with the commencement of a shift from English to Sinhalese and Tamil as the languages of instruction by about 1960. The Sinhalese were the chief beneficiaries of the steep climb in enrolment. Between 1959 and 1963 the number of Sinhalese stu-

their ability to succeed through the use of English. As a minority numerically predominant in only a small part of the island, many of whose members had migrated to the Sinhalese-speaking South in search of employment, the Tamils presumably saw slight advantage in the abandonment of English.

Although a large section of the community was educated in Tamil, the Tamils were not divided by a language barrier to the same extent as were the Sinhalese. Neither the economic and social distance nor the cultural gap separating the English-educated from the vernacular-educated appears to have been as wide among the Tamils as among the Sinhalese. The social conservatism of the Tamil community probably contributed toward minimizing the divisive effect of English education and Westernization. Consequently, the social discontents which bred the swabhasha movement in the South were less pronounced in the Tamil-speaking North. Although after independence few Tamil political leaders actively opposed change in the official language, most were content to allow the Sinhalese to initiate the main demands and limited their role to asking for the Tamil language whatever gains were made for Sinhalese.

---

dents more than doubled (increasing from 1,983 to 4,200), while the number of Tamil students grew by only about 20 per cent. Thus, by 1963 Sinhalese constituted about 74 per cent and Tamils about 22 per cent of the student body. Data on university enrolment by community are from Ceylon, Department of Census and Statistics, *Statistical Abstract of Ceylon* for 1954-1964 (Colombo: Government Press, 1954-1965).

CHAPTER IV

The triumph of Sinhalese-only

The official language issue arose primarily as a contest between swabhasha and English. Eventually, however, the demand for swabhasha among the Sinhalese majority was transformed into insistence on Sinhalese as the sole official language, and the controversy began to shift from the question of swabhasha or English to that of both Sinhalese and Tamil or Sinhalese only. The language agitation retained strong elements of protest against the privileges and cultural estrangement of the English-educated, but with the growing sentiment for Sinhalese as the only official language, communal rivalry rapidly assumed central importance. The official language question inherently possessed great potential for an explosive clash between communities. Language was fundamental to the identity of each community and intimately bound up with the community's distinctive culture and way of life. The issue became the principal focus of mounting communal rivalry and tensions.

"Swabhasha" had been a marvelously ambiguous slogan for rallying political support. Until the advanced stages of the movement little thought was given to its exact meaning in a multi-lingual state. To the majority Sinhalese community, the term could stand for Sinhalese, the predominant language of Ceylon. To the minority Tamil community, it could mean Sinhalese and Tamil, the languages of the Ceylonese people. While the accepted policy of all major political groups for nearly a decade after 1944 was that swabhasha included both Sinhalese and Tamil, few considered what the relationship between the languages was to be. Sinhalese might be used in the Sinhalese-speaking areas and Tamil in the Tamil-speaking areas, or both languages might be used throughout the island. S. W. R. D. Bandaranaike later observed of the period: "Our minds were really fixed at that time on the question of English *versus* Swabasha. We did not bring our minds to bear, maybe it was a fault on our part, on the question of Sinhalese *versus* Tamil."[1]

Tamil leaders, then mostly professionals and public servants whose careers had been in Colombo, insisted that absolute equality of status or "parity" should exist between Sinhalese and Tamil throughout the island. Tamil is the predominant language in only two of nine provinces, and if Sinhalese alone were to be used in the Sinhalese-speaking provinces the opportunities for Tamil-educated public servants would be greatly curtailed.[2] As the eventual displacement of English began to seem assured, discussion tended to shift from "swabhasha" to "parity," and a Sinhalese reaction against the equal status of languages implied by parity began to develop. Parity was being vigorously championed by G. G. Ponnambalam, who had taken the lead in urging on the Soulbury Commission the "fifty-fifty" scheme to deprive the Sinhalese of a legislative majority. To many Sinhalese, the campaign for parity represented a renewed attempt to preserve a position of advantage and secure an unwarranted place for the Tamil minority relative to the Sinhalese majority. The idea that Sinhalese alone might replace English had always been present. The original resolution submitted to the State Council in 1944 had specified only Sinhalese as the official language until it was amended to include Tamil. Sinhalese demands for swabhasha were gradually replaced by demands for Sinhalese as the sole official language of Ceylon.

Competition for public service employment

An important role in the rise of the demand for Sinhalese as the only official language was played by communal competition for government employment and Sinhalese resentment of disproportionate Tamil strength in the public service. With the availability of English education as a result of the early opening of missionary schools and the paucity of alternative employment opportunities in the arid North, the Tamils had turned in large numbers to the public service. The Tamil areas did not possess the natural conditions which had created economic

1. S. W. R. D. Bandaranaike, *Towards a New Era* (Colombo: Department of Information, 1961), p. 388.
2. See I. D. S. Weerawardana, *Ceylon General Election, 1956* (Colombo: M. D. Gunasena & Co., Ltd., 1960), pp. 5-8.

opportunities in the South. Education became one of the principal economic resources of the North, and English-educated youths the leading
export of Jaffna. In 1911, 4.9 per cent of the Ceylon Tamil males
were literate in English, compared with 3.5 per cent of the Low-
Country Sinhalese and only 0.7 per cent of Kandyan Sinhalese males.[3]
The Tamils similarly predominated in the occupational classification of
government service and professions in the census of 1911. Among Ceylon Tamils, 5.1 per cent were included within this classification, along
with 3.6 per cent of the Low-Country Sinhalese and 1.3 per cent of the
Kandyan Sinhalese.[4]

Tamils from the North entered the clerical grades of the public
service in substantial numbers, and as the administrative and professional grades progressively opened to Ceylonese, Tamils also secured
a proportion of posts in the higher bureaucratic levels greater than their
proportion of the population.[5] Jaffna Tamils had crossed to Malaya to
obtain public service posts until 1922, when appointments in the Malay-
an government were closed to them. At about the same time, the expansion of estate agriculture, mining, and trade slackened in the Sinhalese areas. With growing numbers of Sinhalese receiving English educations and aspiring to white-collar employment, the attention of the
Sinhalese increasingly turned to the public service. By 1930, the proportion of Sinhalese in the clerical and higher grades of the bureaucracy
had begun to rise. However, a decade before independence Tamils continued to hold about twice as great a proportion of pensionable public
service posts as their proportion of the population. Sinhalese held less
than three times as many of these positions as Tamils, although they
were more than six times more numerous in the population of Ceylon.[6]
In 1946, the select Ceylon Civil Service contained nearly half as many
Tamils as Sinhalese, and the Judicial Service included two-thirds as
many Tamils as Sinhalese.[7]

As Sinhalese increasingly sought public service appointments, the

3. E. B. Denham, *Ceylon at the Census of 1911* (Colombo: Government Printer,
1912), p. 434.
4. *Ibid.*, p. 479.
5. S. J. Tambiah, "Ethnic Representation in Ceylon's Higher Administrative Services,
1870-1946," *University of Ceylon Review*, XIII, 2-3 (April-July, 1955), 130-133.
6. Soulbury Report, p. 49.
7. Tambiah, "Ethnic Representation . . . ," p. 133.

feeling developed that the opportunities for Sinhalese aspirants were reduced by the prior establishment of the Tamils in the bureaucracy. The severe limitation on opportunities imposed by stringent economic conditions sharpened rivalry for the meager existing opportunities. With the demand for government jobs outrunning their availability, communal identification and solidarity led to concern with communal proportions in the public service and support for one's "own people" striving to gain entrance. Governor Caldecott in 1938 described the unique role of competition for public service jobs in accentuating communal rivalry in Ceylon. He contended that "the Public Service looms far too prominently in the thoughts and attentions of the Islanders," resulting in

the desire of every parent to see a son get a Government job, and intense jealousy if that job falls to somebody of a different family, caste, or race. The extent to which this obsession obtains may be illustrated by a proposal which was made to me, though not in any official representations, that appointments to Clerkships should be by rotation between the races. I have no doubt whatever that a great deal of the communalism that is so unfortunately rampant derives directly from competition and jealousy about Government appointments.[8]

After communal passions inflamed by the language controversy had swept the island, a Tamil senator charged:

University graduates and people like that are the cause of all the trouble—not the vast mass of the Sinhalese people. It is these men, these middle-class unemployed seeking employment, who are jealous of the fact that a few Tamils occupy seats of office in the Government—these are the people who have gone round the country-side, rousing the masses and creating this problem.[9]

The Sinhalese, aroused to heightened consciousness of their ethnic identity by the Buddhist revival and the social and political reform movements at the beginning of the century, increasingly resented the apparent Tamil entrenchment in the public service. In political debate, the disproportion of Tamils in government employment was frequently

8. Great Britain, Colonial Office, *Correspondence Relating to the Constitution of Ceylon,* Cmd. 5910 (London: His Majesty's Stationery Office, 1938), p. 20.

9. Ceylon, Senate, *Parliamentary Debates (Hansard),* Vol. 10, cols. 576-577. That middle-class occupational rivalry was the major cause of the growth of communalism is argued by G. C. Mendis, *Ceylon Today and Yesterday* (2nd ed. rev.; Colombo: Associated Newspapers of Ceylon, Ltd., 1963), pp. 128-136.

exaggerated remarkably.[10] The Sinhalese advocates of swabhasha were not anxious to drive the English-educated Sinhalese from the public service only to turn it over to the Tamils. If Sinhalese became the only language of government, it was felt, an advantage in access to public service employment would be obtained by the Sinhalese, which would correct the imbalance created under colonial rule and compensate the Sinhalese for past injustices.

Sinhalese language attitudes and emotions

Emotions similar to those which generated the demand for swabhasha helped lead the language movement into the exclusive demand for Sinhalese-only. Great importance was attached to the prestige and status accorded by government recognition as the "official language." This recognition was looked upon by those who wished to revitalize the Sinhalese language as having almost miraculous powers for reversing the fortunes of the language. Many Sinhalese concerned for the survival of their ancestral language believed that an equal official status for the Sinhalese and Tamil languages would lead to the eventual triumph of Tamil. Just as the Ceylon Tamils feared political domination by the majority Sinhalese, the Sinhalese believed themselves to be a besieged minority in linguistic, religious, and cultural matters. While the Tamils feared the Sinhalese preponderance on the island, the Sinhalese feared cultural submergence by the thirty million Tamil-speaking people across the narrow Palk Strait in India. Sinhalese argued that six million Sinhalese in Ceylon were the world's only speakers of the Sinhalese language and representatives of Sinhalese culture. The Tamil language, in contrast, would exist as a living language regardless of its fate in Ceylon. If the Tamil language, with its ancient literature and centers of learning and publishing in India, were given equal status with Sinhalese, the Sinhalese language might be saved from English only to be smothered by Tamil. S. W. R. D. Bandaranaike, describing these fears, claimed the majority of the Sinhalese people

felt that as the Tamil language was spoken by so many millions in other countries, and possessed a much wider literature and as the Tamil-speaking people

10. A figure as high as 80 per cent was sometimes cited. E.g., Ceylon, House of Representatives, *Parliamentary Debates (Hansard)*, Vol. 24, col. 320.

had every means of propagating their literature and culture, it would have an advantage over Sinhalese which was spoken only by a few million people in this country. They felt that not only in the Northern and Eastern Provinces was there a majority of Tamils, but that there was a large number of Tamil people in the Sinhalese provinces . . . and that . . . all this would create a situation when the natural tendency would be for the use of Sinhalese to shrink and probably in the course of time almost to reach the point of elimination.[11]

The Sinhalese-only proponents argued that Sinhalese was the language of the overwhelming majority—nearly 70 per cent of the inhabitants of the island and, more importantly, 80 per cent of the citizens of Ceylon—and that the size of the Tamil minority was not sufficient to justify equal treatment for the Tamil language. It was held to be only reasonable that the minorities accept the predominant position of the Sinhalese. Two official languages, it was asserted, would divide the country, as neither Sinhalese nor Tamils would have any incentive to learn the language of the other. Tamil insistence on parity throughout the island was taken as a sign of Tamil arrogance in demanding for their language a status equal to that of the much more numerous Sinhalese, reminiscent of the earlier "fifty-fifty" demand. It was claimed that two official languages were unnecessary and undesirable and that the rightful position of the majority, denied under colonial rule, should be restored by declaring Sinhalese the sole official language.

The Sinhalese-only campaign aroused a powerful response among the ordinary Sinhalese people, far removed from rivalry over urban white-collar jobs. The individual Sinhalese tended to identify his fortunes with those of his language and to see the status of his language reflected in his own sense of dignity and self-respect. The Sinhalese-only agitation and the related Buddhist claims effectively galvanized the lingering sense of identification on the basis of language and religion. The strong bond of communal solidarity drew the Sinhalese behind the call for Sinhalese-only. To the Sinhalese, the language movement became a symbol of their resurgence and self-assertion as a unique and proud people.

In 1953, the Official Languages Commission, which had studied the proposed transition from English to swabhasha, issued its final report. A rider attached to the report by the commission chairman, E. A. L.

11. *Ibid.*, Vol. 24, col. 843.

Wijeyewardene, asserted that "the replacement of English by Swabhasha would have been very much easier if instead of two Swabhasha Languages as Official Languages one alone had been accepted."[12] The following year the same man as chairman of a Commission on Higher Education in the National Languages, in a rider to a report of that commission, warned of grave disadvantages faced by Sinhalese students because few educational materials existed in Sinhalese, while materials in Tamil were available from South India. He concluded: "Of course, this difficulty will not arise, if there is only one official national language."[13] This represented the first quasi-official recognition of the mounting Sinhalese-only demands.

The political contest

The idea of Sinhalese as the only official language was gaining momentum among political parties, all of which had previously advocated substitution of both Sinhalese and Tamil for English. In 1953, the Sri Lanka Freedom party undertook a re-examination of its language policy. A committee charged with studying the question reported in favor of Sinhalese-only, and the party's 1955 annual conference approved the change.[14] A small Marxist group called the Viplavakari Lanka Sama Samaja party also declared for Sinhalese as the sole official language. Bhasha Peramuna (Language Front) organizations were springing up throughout the South to work for Sinhalese-only. The Lanka Sama Samaja party (LSSP) and the Communist party maintained adherence to parity, but suffered desertions and revolts in their ranks. Meetings staged by these two parties in support of parity were attacked and broken up by mobs of Sinhalese-only enthusiasts in late 1955.[15]

The swelling tide of Sinhalese-only sentiment created a difficult problem of language policy for the UNP. The Sinhalese-only movement was apparently attracting tremendous political strength, and the party

12. *Final Report of the Official Languages Commission* (Sessional Paper XXII, 1953), p. 26.
13. *Interim Report of the Commission on Higher Education in National Languages* (Sessional Paper XXI, 1954), p. 6.
14. House, *Debates*, Vol. 24, cols. 840-841.
15. Weerawardana, *Ceylon General Election, 1956*, pp. 11-14, 22-23; Leslie Goonewardene, *A Short History of the Lanka Sama Samaja Party* (Colombo: Lanka Sama Samaja Party, 1960), pp. 53-54.

would be required to face the polls again by 1957. However, the UNP was firmly committed to a policy of parity for Sinhalese and Tamil. Although its leadership was largely Sinhalese and most of its support came from Sinhalese areas, it had always been to some extent a multi-communal party and contained a small Tamil membership. The leadership and articulate support of the party had come from the English-educated, Westernized commercial and professional segment of society in which communal sentiments were attenuated. Each Cabinet formed under UNP auspices since 1947 had contained two Tamil ministers. D. S. Senanayake, the first leader of the UNP, generally seems to have held the respect and confidence of the Tamils. In a 1948 debate, he claimed:

There is no question of one community being inferior or superior to any other community. All people have got equal rights. . . . If I failed to appreciate the arguments of my Friend when he appealed on behalf of one community, it was because I do not differentiate between one community and another. I treat them all alike.[16]

G. G. Ponnambalam served in the Cabinet, and the Tamil Congress supported the UNP Government from 1949 until 1953. When Sir John Kotelawala became prime minister and dropped Ponnambalam from the Cabinet, the Tamil Congress went into opposition but some of its members broke away and joined the UNP. Kotelawala was thought to be sympathetic to minority interests during his premiership.[17] He once said in a radio message, "We . . . cannot afford to think in terms of narrow sectarianism, for, as I have often said, the country belongs to us all whether we are Burghers, Muslims, Tamils, or Sinhalese."[18] While individual UNP members were not necessarily less subject to communalist sentiments than adherents of other parties and contradictory behavior by party officials and supporters was not unknown, the

16. House, *Debates*, Vol. 2, cols. 3497-3498. See the tribute to D. S. Senanayake paid by a Tamil M.P. during an acrimonious exchange on the language issue in 1960. *Ibid.*, Vol. 38, col. 342. The D. S. Senanayake and UNP attitude of communal co-operation and equality did not, however, extend to the Indian Tamils. Some UNP opponents have been skeptical of the depth of mutual trust existing between the UNP leadership and the Ceylon Tamils. For example, see Doric de Souza, "Parliamentary Democracy in Ceylon," *Young Socialist* (Colombo), I, 3 (Oct.-Dec., 1961), 127.

17. J. L. Fernando, *Three Prime Ministers of Ceylon: An 'Inside Story'* (Colombo: M. D. Gunasena & Co., Ltd., 1963), pp. 84-89. Fernando records Kotelawala's personal disapproval of adopting Sinhalese as the only official language. *Ibid.*, p. 87.

18. *U.N.P. Journal*, Jan. 8, 1954.

party had developed the habit of taking a multi-communal outlook. A Tamil minister and founder of the UNP claimed the party "was formed with a view to bringing all the communities together, with a view to making it a forum where all people belonging to this country could discuss matters and arrive at decisions irrespective of their belonging to a certain race or religion or speak[ing] in different languages."[19]

In the face of a rising tempo of agitation for Sinhalese-only, the UNP leadership insisted that the party would stand by its commitment to both languages. As Sinhalese-only sentiment spread in the South, Prime Minister Kotelawala attempted to reassure the Tamils by visiting Jaffna in September, 1954. His reported promise to amend the constitution to guarantee parity for Sinhalese and Tamil produced an instantaneous and vocal reaction in the South. The effect of Kotelawala's statement seems to have been to harden Sinhalese determination to make Sinhalese the sole official language.[20] The UNP was thereafter on the defensive on the language question. With pressure mounting within the party for a change in language policy, UNP ministers and members of Parliament were allowed to voice their individual sentiments on the language issue. The result was that although the party's official policy still called for parity, most of the UNP's Sinhalese ministers and M.P.'s were publicly advocating Sinhalese-only, while Tamil party members continued to plead for parity.[21]

At the end of 1955, the UNP leaders decided to bow to the mounting pressure for Sinhalese-only, and attempted to dramatize the shift in policy by announcing an early dissolution of Parliament and a general election to secure a mandate for the change.[22] The effect was destroyed, however, by premature disclosure of UNP intentions and the appearance of insincerity and opportunism in the abrupt reversal. In January, 1956, the UNP's Tamil M.P.'s resigned from the party. The following month the party's annual conference was offered and ap-

19. House, *Debates*, Vol. 23, cols. 1857-1858.
20. Bandaranaike was of the opinion that the explosive nature of subsequent language passions was the result of Kotelawala's reported statement. *Ibid.*, Vol. 24, cols. 842-845. Kotelawala claimed that his statement had been misconstrued. *Ibid.*, Vol. 21, cols. 485-486.
21. Weerawardana, *Ceylon General Election, 1956*, pp. 13-14.
22. For discussions of the calculations which prompted the UNP shift in policy and decision for an early election, see *ibid.*, pp. 13-19; and Fernando, *Three Prime Ministers*, pp. 81-88.

proved only one resolution—that "Sinhalese alone should be made the State Language of Ceylon."[23]

A few days after the UNP formally joined the Sinhalese-only camp, a coalition called the Mahajana Eksath Peramuna (People's United Front) was formed by the groups previously spearheading the Sinhalese-only movement. The largest and most important of the coalition partners was the Sri Lanka Freedom party led by S. W. R. D. Bandaranaike, who assumed leadership of the MEP. Other components of the MEP coalition were the Viplavakari Lanka Sama Samaja party, the Bhasha Peramuna, and a collection of independents. The MEP adopted a program calling for Sinhalese to be made the only official language immediately. A provision, however, was added: "This will not involve the suppression of such a minority language as Tamil, whose reasonable use will receive due recognition."[24] This gesture toward reducing Tamil fears surpassed the language declaration of the UNP, which had specified no concession for Tamil.

Prior to the formation of the MEP coalition, the SLFP had entered into a "no-contest" pact with the LSSP and the Communist party to avoid contesting the same electorates and thus splitting the anti-UNP vote. For the first time since its founding the UNP was faced by a relatively united opposition. From the standpoint of language policy, the somewhat equivocal situation was created wherein the SLFP was allied in a coalition on the basis of mutual enthusiasm for Sinhalese-only, but was at the same time tied by a no-contest pact to parties supporting parity of languages. This arrangement was directed against the UNP which, although a recent convert, was pledged to Sinhalese-only.

The UNP and MEP contested electorates only in the Sinhalese areas, while the Tamil Congress and Federal party, formed in 1949 after a split in the Tamil Congress, limited their efforts to the Tamil areas. Only the LSSP and the Communist party offered candidates in both Sinhalese and Tamil constituencies. With both the UNP and MEP proclaiming their support for Sinhalese-only, the campaign in the Sin-

23. *United National Party Eighth Annual Conference and Mass Rally* (Colombo: United National Party, [1956]), unpaged; Sir John Kotelawala, "Prime Minister's Speech, United National Party Eighth Annual Conference, 1956" (mimeographed; Colombo, 1956), pp. 2-5.
24. *Joint Programme of the Mahajana Eksath Peramuna* (Colombo: Mahajana Eksath Peramuna, 1956), p. 2.

halese areas tended to develop into a contest over who would be most sincere and determined in carrying out the change in official language.[25] The UNP fared badly in this competition, not only because of the questionable sincerity of its belated change in policy, but also because of its popular identification with the English language and its earlier apparently dilatory approach to language reform.

Closely intertwined with the Sinhalese-only movement was a growth of Buddhist political militancy.[26] Many links connected discontent with the state of Buddhism and the desire for Sinhalese as the sole official language. The religion and the language were both integral elements of traditional Sinhalese civilization that had suffered under Western intrusions. Although Sinhalese Christians were found at all levels of society, the urban English-speaking middle class was disproportionately Christian, and the strongholds of Buddhism tended to be in the sectors of society least touched by modernizing developments and Western influences. Often, the attack on the dominance of the Westernized middle class was simultaneously a class revolt against exclusive privilege, a traditionalist reaction against the adoption of an alien language and culture, and a religious hostility toward a Christian or secular outlook and indifference to Buddhism. Buddhist dissatisfactions were brought into sharp relief by the approach of the Buddha Jayanti, the 2,500th anni-

25. Weerawardana, *Ceylon General Election, 1956,* p. 104.

26. The attempt here is to examine the impact of Buddhist political activism only as it relates more or less directly to the language controversy and rivalry of the Sinhalese and Tamil communities. A comprehensive discussion of religion and politics in Ceylon would tend to lead away from the central concern of this study. While Buddhism was a focus of Sinhalese self-identification, as mentioned earlier, and the Buddhist discontents and Sinhalese language demands tended to merge particularly at the time of the 1956 election, Sinhalese communal aspirations and Sinhalese-Tamil rivalry are not inseparable from or completely explicable in terms of the Buddhist ferment and growing activism. The most urgent protests and demands made in the name of the Sinhalese Buddhists are frequently directed against Sinhalese Christians, not Tamil Hindus. E.g., see Robert N. Kearney, "Sinhalese Nationalism and Social Conflict in Ceylon," *Pacific Affairs,* XXXVII, 2 (Summer, 1964), 125-136. An example of Buddhist claims directed primarily toward the exclusion of the Christians, the majority of whom are Sinhalese, rather than the predominantly Hindu Tamil ethnic community, appeared in a recommendation for the establishment of quotas to regulate admission to the university and appointment to the public service made in 1961. The recommendation specifically rejected "race" (i.e., community) as the basis of quotas in favor of religion, indicating a concern less with relative Sinhalese-Tamil opportunities than with Buddhist opportunities relative to Christians (Sinhalese or other) who had previously obtained a disproportionate share of university educations and public service jobs. The recommendation appears in *Final Report of the National Education Commission, 1961* (Sessional Paper XVII, 1962), pp. 152-153.

versary of the death of the Buddha, to be observed in 1956. Preparations for the observances focused attention on the state of Buddhism and led to an upsurge in Buddhist religious feeling and sense of identity. The Buddha Jayanti reinforced the link between the Buddhist discontents and Sinhalese linguistic and nationalist sentiments. The celebrations were hailed as commemorating a "unique three-fold event"—the founding of Buddhism, the settlement of Ceylon, and the origin of the Sinhalese people.[27] Virtually all the Buddhist militants who streamed into the election campaign were also champions of Sinhalese-only.

A report entitled *The Betrayal of Buddhism*, published by the influential All-Ceylon Buddhist Congress on the eve of the campaign, was largely responsible for steering inchoate Buddhist discontent into political action directed against the UNP. The report depicted the plight of Buddhism as primarily a consequence of the persecution, discrimination, and hostility of Western colonialism, which it claimed had been perpetuated by the post-independence UNP Governments.[28] Echoing the traditionalist attack on middle-class estrangement of a half-century earlier, the report charged that although Ceylon became free in 1948, "the value of this freedom was vitiated by the fact that those who came to the helm in the country's affairs were mainly people completely dominated by an alien outlook and values, and estranged from their national history and culture."[29]

Concern for the condition and future prospects of Buddhism and the Sinhalese language and grievances stemming from the decline of their own status and functions drew many bhikkhus into partisan activity. In traditional Sinhalese society, the bhikkhus played an important role in the life of the community and were accorded great respect by the people and rulers alike. The difficulties encountered by Buddhism during the colonial period had harmed the bhikkhus' position and tended to isolate the sangha in the villages away from the change and modernization occurring in the urban areas. The growth of secular education deprived the sangha of its traditional educational role and weakened its

27. D. C. Vijayavardhana, *The Revolt in the Temple* (Colombo: Sinha Publications, 1953), p. 25.
28. These accusations were asserted or implied at many points throughout the report. See Buddhist Committee of Inquiry, *The Betrayal of Buddhism* (Balangoda, Ceylon: Dharmavijaya Press, 1956), pp. 13-14, 37, 83.
29. *Ibid.*, p. 99.

ties with the people. The language agitation held considerable appeal for many bhikkhus. Few had learned English or acquired Western education. As the traditional custodians of Sinhalese literature and scholarship, the bhikkhus were disturbed by the inroads of English and the atrophy of Sinhalese. Most of the politically active bhikkhus energetically worked for the MEP and attacked the UNP on the language and religious issues. The principal vehicle for bhikkhu political activity was the Eksath Bhikkhu Peramuna (Bhikkhu United Front), which was among the most vociferous and uncompromising champions of Sinhalese-only.[30]

The election in April, 1956, resulted in an astounding victory for the MEP coalition. The MEP, which had been hard pressed to field a total of sixty candidates, captured fifty-one seats, an absolute majority in the House of Representatives. The mighty UNP, which won fifty-four seats in the preceding election, was able to hold only eight seats, insufficient to form the official opposition. A number of factors contributed to the UNP debacle. The election climaxed several years of growing popular disenchantment with the party. Since its victory in 1952, the UNP had appeared successively to be oppressive, complacent, corrupt, and unprincipled. Tactical blunders and inept leadership magnified its difficulties. While it is impossible to isolate the impact of the language issue, the election nonetheless seemed to demonstrate the tremendous political force capable of being generated by emotions and interests linked to language.[31]

S. W. R. D. Bandaranaike was the principal architect of the MEP victory. Although an Oxford-educated scion of a highly Westernized Christian family of the low-country aristocracy whose godfather had been the British colonial governor, Bandaranaike displayed an early appreciation of ethnic, linguistic, and religious identifications. On his return from Oxford in 1925, he apologized to an assembled delegation of

30. On Buddhist activism and the EBP in the campaign, see Weerawardana, *Ceylon General Election, 1956*, pp. 109-114, 143-150; and W. Howard Wriggins, *Ceylon: Dilemmas of a New Nation* (Princeton: Princeton University Press, 1960), pp. 206-207, 342-348. For the sources of Buddhist discontents, see Mendis, *Ceylon Today and Yesterday*, pp. 145-166.

31. For more detailed examinations of the 1956 election, see the excellent analyses contained in Weerawardana, *Ceylon General Election, 1956*; and Wriggins, *Ceylon: Dilemmas of a New Nation*, chap. ix. Weerawardana appears to attribute a somewhat more dominant role to the language issue.

neighbors and family retainers for his inability to address them in Sinhalese, but declared: "I can assure you that my heart is Sinhalese to the core."[32] In the next few years he studied the Sinhalese language, became a Buddhist, and entered politics. From the days of the Sinhala Maha Sabha devoted to promoting the solidarity of the Sinhalese, Bandaranaike had tended to speak in terms of communities and espouse essentially Sinhalese causes and goals. In justifying the existence of the Sabha as an exclusively Sinhalese political organization, he asserted in 1939: "We feel that true friendship and co-operation must come rather from mutual understanding of each other's differences than by a denial that such differences exist at all."[33] He became a prominent spokesman for Buddhist discontents and an advocate first of swabhasha and later of Sinhalese-only. He commended to an Asian socialist conference in 1956 "a combination of democratic Socialism and religio-cultural ideas, which cannot be divorced, especially in Asia, from any movement any time."[34]

The UNP had never developed an effective mass organization[35] and attempted to rely for articulation with the rural population on the intermediation of eminent and wealthy landowning families of the locality, village headmen who were generally selected from prominent local families, and in some cases prosperous local traders and merchants. When Bandaranaike left the UNP and founded the SLFP in 1951, he was able to create an alternative avenue for mobilizing rural support as a result of changes which were occurring in the villages. Small village traders, teachers in the vernacular schools, minor landowners, and *ayurvedic* physicians had begun to challenge the dominance of the prominent families and to secure a foothold in the rural local government bodies, the village committees. Although these new aspirants to village leadership occupied a social position based generally on individual achievement rather than inherited status, they were less exposed to

32. S. W. R. D. Bandaranaike, *Speeches and Writings* (Colombo: Department of Broadcasting and Information, 1963), pp. 82-83.
33. Bandaranaike, *Towards a New Era*, p. 51.
34. Quoted in Alex Josey, *Socialism in Asia* (Singapore: Donald Moore, 1957), p. 51.
35. Indications of the weaknesses of the UNP's system of branch organizations and links with the public, particularly in the rural areas, appeared frequently in party publications prior to the 1956 election. E.g. a statement by J. L. Kotelawala, in U. A. Jayasundera (ed.), *United National Party Independence Souvenir, 1951* (Colombo: United National Party, 1951), p. 168; and *U.N.P. Journal*, Dec. 4, 1953, and Sept. 3, 1954.

modernizing influences and tended to be more traditional in their outlook and values than those they sought to displace. They were Sinhalese-educated and Buddhists and were strongly attracted by the Sinhalese-only movement and the Buddhist demands.[36]

Bandaranaike's liaison with the rural population was greatly facilitated by his service as minister of local government from 1936 until
his resignation from the Cabinet in 1951. For some fifteen years he was
in frequent contact with village functionaries, elective and appointive,
throughout the island. Through this channel he seems to have maintained much closer contact with the moods, desires, and fears of the
rural villagers than did most of his colleagues in the government. He
built up a following among the village committeemen which by 1956
became a firm base of support for the SLFP and the MEP coalition.
The social, cultural, and political estrangement of the urban-oriented,
middle-class UNP leadership from the rural population made it possible for Bandaranaike to drive the UNP from power by harnessing the
frustrations and grievances which had found expression in the language
and religious issues.

The passage of Sinhalese-only legislation

The first legislative enactment of the new MEP Government following the election was an Official Language Act declaring "the Sinhala
Language shall be the one official language of Ceylon."[37] The bill was
introduced on June 5 and passed by the House of Representatives on
June 14, 1956, with the MEP and UNP members of Parliament voting
for the bill and the LSSP and Communist M.P.'s and the representatives of the Tamil areas opposing it.[38] The act did little more than declare Sinhalese to be the sole official language and confer authority for
implementation on the responsible minister (the prime minister). Where
immediate adoption of Sinhalese was deemed impractical, the minister
was authorized to employ the language or languages then in use as long
as necessary until December 31, 1960.

To the Tamils, the rapid mobilization of Sinhalese-only sentiment

36. See Mendis, *Ceylon Today and Yesterday*, pp. 137-144.
37. Official Language Act, No. 33 of 1956. The text of the act is contained in
Appendix I.
38. House, *Debates*, Vol. 24, col. 1924.

in the South, climaxed by the unqualified declaration of Sinhalese as
the sole official language of Ceylon, appeared to be the realization of
their worst fears regarding the intentions of the Sinhalese majority.
The fact that for the first time since independence not a single Tamil
was included in the Cabinet heightened their apprehension. The adoption of Sinhalese as the official language without recognition of Tamil
seemed to members of the Tamil community to reduce them to a state
of inferiority and to cast doubt on their full membership in the polity.[39]
If Tamil were relegated to an inferior position, it was feared, the language would decline in Ceylon and with it the distinctive culture of the
Ceylon Tamils.[40] During the debate on the official language bill, Ponnambalam argued: "The imposition of Sinhalese as the sole official language of this country must inevitably and inexorably put an end, even
if that is not your real objective today, to the Tamil nation and the
Tamil people as such."[41] Another Tamil political leader later charged
that "the moment the Sinhala Only Act was passed in this country, the
country was divided into two groups. The country was divided into the
Sinhalese-speaking people and the Tamil-speaking people."[42]

Spiraling communal tensions and violence

Communal tensions generated by the official language controversy
rapidly spiraled into incendiarism and violence after the 1956 election.
Repeated appeals to language and communal sentiments inflamed popular passions, making virtually impossible a reconciliation of conflicting
Sinhalese and Tamil claims through reasoned accommodation and compromise and creating an atmosphere of disorder and hostility that was
readily exploited by fanatics, adventurers, and *goondas*. The rapid
growth of communal antagonisms in the two years following passage
of the Official Language Act prompted an M.P. to observe:

[T]he political situation in this country is such that consciously or uncon-
sciously everyone is beginning to look at things from a communal angle. . . .
People who have never been communalists have become communalists and

39. E.g., *ibid.*, Vol. 39, col. 410; Senate, *Debates*, Vol. 10, cols. 571-627.
40. See Xavier S. Thani Nayagam, "Tamil Culture—Its Past, Its Present and Its
Future with Special Reference to Ceylon," *Tamil Culture* (Madras), IV, 4 (Oct.,
1955), 341-364.
41. House, *Debates*, Vol. 24, col. 939.
42. *Ibid.*, Vol. 38, col. 559.

those who have been moderates have become extremists while extremists have become incorrigible fanatics.[43]

The victorious MEP coalition in 1956 had aggregated a wide assortment of protests and discontents, and the election campaign had unleashed powerful emotions and stimulated extravagant expectations. The new Government soon found itself beset by frequently immoderate, unrestrained, and contradictory demands from its former election supporters. Many Tamils had professed satisfaction at the MEP victory over the UNP because of the coalition's promise to provide for the "reasonable use" of Tamil.[44] However, the inclusion of a section defining the use of Tamil in the original draft of the official language bill encountered impassioned opposition from Sinhalese-only enthusiasts who had been militant partisans of the MEP during the election campaign. The Eksath Bhikkhu Peramuna staged demonstrations, and a prominent Sinhalese-only champion and MEP supporter fasted on the steps of the Parliament building in protest. In the face of these pressures and growing public excitement, the Cabinet dropped the provisions for Tamil from the bill. An MEP minister later confessed that "when we were on the point of bringing in a set of legislation [defining the position of Tamil] as required by our Manifesto . . . extremists, opportunists, people who wanted to create chaos . . . took steps to start an agitation. Action was postponed."[45] The first communal violence flared as the official language bill was being debated in Parliament. A demonstration against the bill staged by the Federal party, which emerged from the 1956 election as the principal Tamil party, was broken up and the demonstrators and other Tamils were assaulted by a mob of Sinhalese-only champions. Simultaneously, communal rioting erupted in the east-coast Gal Oya colonization settlement where Sinhalese and Tamil colonists lived side by side.[46] Tamil demands became more insistent, and Sinhalese-only proponents became more uncompromising and aggressive.

43. *Ibid.*, Vol. 33, cols. 1746-1747.

44. E.g., Senate, *Debates*, Vol. 10, cols. 619-620.

45. House, *Debates*, Vol. 31, col. 734. See also Wriggins, *Ceylon: Dilemmas of a New Nation*, pp. 259-261.

46. A government commission investigating the riots recorded receiving reports of "various acts of outrage and violence," but concluded that publication of its findings after the rioting had subsided might lead to renewed communal tensions. *Interim Report of the Commission of Inquiry into the Outbreaks of Civil Disturbance in the Eastern Province* (Sessional Paper III, 1957), pp. 2-3.

In August, a Federal party conference issued an ultimatum that if the party's language and other demands were not met within one year the party would launch a *satyagraha* or non-violent direct-action campaign to achieve its aims. As the date of the scheduled *satyagraha* neared, Prime Minister Bandaranaike began discussions with the Federalist leaders which culminated on July 26, 1957, in the drafting and signing of a formal written agreement, popularly known as the Bandaranaike-Chelvanayakam Pact. On the language question, a formula was agreed upon for legislation containing "recognition of Tamil as the language of a national minority" and providing that "the language of administration of the Northern and Eastern Provinces should be Tamil." Regional councils with powers relating to agriculture, education, and other matters including the selection of colonists for government-sponsored colonization schemes were to be established to meet Federalist demands for Tamil political autonomy and an end to Sinhalese colonization of Tamil areas. The pact concluded with the statement that because of the agreement, the Federal party was abandoning its planned *satyagraha*.[47] The provisions of the accord repeatedly reappeared in later negotiations between Sinhalese and Tamil politicians.

Bandaranaike believed that the agreement had resolved the deadlock between Sinhalese and Tamils on the language issue. The settlement, he avowed, would "safeguard the position of the Sinhalese while, at the same time, meet reasonably the fears of the Tamils."[48] A Federalist leader said that in the pact negotiations Bandaranaike recognized that "our party represented the masses, the heart of the Tamil people, and he stated that his party too, the S.L.F.P. represented the heart of the Sinhalese people. Therefore he felt that there must be some kind of agreement."[49]

Vociferous opposition to the agreement immediately developed. Uncompromising Sinhalese-only advocates violently attacked the accord as a betrayal of the Sinhalese community. The militant Eksath Bhikkhu Peramuna threatened to launch a *satyagraha* of its own unless the pact

47. The text of the pact is contained in Appendix II.
48. S. W. R. D. Bandaranaike, "Message by the Prime Minister," in *Śrī Laṅkā Nidahas Pakṣaya Sāṁvatsarika Kalāpaya, 1958* [*Sri Lanka Freedom Party Annual Number, 1958*] (Colombo: Sri Lanka Freedom Party, 1958), p. 15.
49. House, *Debates*, Vol. 45, col. 2008.

was repudiated.[50] The UNP denounced the pact as a communal division of the island. While opposition to the pact flourished in the South, Tamils were reacting to what they felt to be affronts of the Sinhalese Government. Tamils had protested the adornment of automobile license plates with the word *śrī* in Sinhalese. In March, 1958, busses of the state-owned Ceylon Transport Board bearing the *śrī* license plates were sent to Jaffna. A campaign was begun by the Federalists to obliterate the Sinhalese lettering with tar and substitute Tamil lettering. In reply, street signs and shop signboards in Tamil were tarred over in Colombo. Under heavy pressure from opponents of the pact as communal passions rose, Bandaranaike used the Federal party activities in the North as justification for abrogating the pact.[51] He handed a written repudiation of the pact to an assemblage of bhikkhus and others demonstrating at his residence. Thereafter, communal tensions swiftly exploded into brutal rioting. A train carrying delegates to a Federal party convention was derailed and the delegates were assaulted. Violence spread quickly as rumors of atrocities circulated. Tamils in the South were beaten or killed and their homes and shops burned. In retaliation, Sinhalese in the North were attacked. Looting, arson, and wanton brutality erupted in many scattered areas. The death toll mounted into the hundreds. Thousands of Tamils were evacuated to the North and Sinhalese to the South.

Bandaranaike hesitated for four days as terror swept the island, then declared an emergency and turned over power to restore law and order to the governor-general. A number of Federal party members and the leader of a small inflammatory Sinhalese party, the Jathika Vimukthi Peramuna (National Liberation Front), were placed under house arrest. The rioting was gradually quelled by stern army and police action.[52] Some of the atmosphere of tension and violence as the holocaust spread across the island was captured in the usually staid annual reports of government agents in charge of districts engulfed by the rioting. The following descriptions were written of the riots in the Colombo and Kurunegala Districts:

50. *Ibid.*, Vol. 31, cols. 25-32; Wiggins, *Ceylon: Dilemmas of a New Nation*, pp. 266-267.

51. See Bandaranaike's explanation, House, *Debates*, Vol. 31, cols. 11-13.

52. A graphic account of the riots is contained in Tarzie Vittachi, *Emergency '58* (London: Andre Deutsch, 1958).

The situation in the [Colombo] District was tense and highly dangerous on the 26th and 27th May. Passing vehicles were stopped and their occupants mercilessly assaulted. Moving trains were halted at several places and the passengers ruthlessly attacked. There were many instances of arson and such brutal scenes as men being burnt alive. Looting was rampant. The Police were helpless against these marauding rioters.[53]

On May 26, 1958, communal tension came to a head in Kurunegala. On the evening of this day rioting started in the bazaar area. Several Tamil shops were attacked and burnt. Looting followed and as a result of the general confusion the Police had to open fire to disperse the mob. Throughout the night of the 26th isolated acts of violence and incendiarism were reported from all parts of the District. On the morning of the 27th feelings again began to run high and might have developed much further but for the promulgation of a state of emergency and the imposition of the curfew. However, the District was then in a state of tension and the Kurunegala Police [station] was flooded with refugees. On the 28th of May, Military assistance was available and this together with the other action taken had the effect of subduing the feeling of tension which hitherto prevailed in an acute form. The refugees problem [w]as gradually settled by escorting them in batches through Puttalam and Anuradhapura to Jaffna.[54]

Shortly after the rioting subsided, a Tamil Language Act intended to define at last the "reasonable use" of Tamil was enacted. The bill came before the House of Representatives while the Federal party M.P.'s were still under detention, and almost the entire opposition walked out of the chamber in protest against consideration of the bill in the absence of the Tamil representatives.[55] The act provided for the use of Tamil in education, public service entrance examinations, and "prescribed administrative purposes" in the Northern and Eastern Provinces. The prime minister was authorized to make regulations to implement the act.[56] More than seven additional years were to pass, however, before the first regulation necessary for the act to have effect was promulgated. Following passage of the act, Bandaranaike explained his formula for restoring communal amity and asserted that the official

53. Report of the government agent, Colombo District, in *Administration Reports of the Government Agents for 1958* (Colombo: Government Press, 1960), pp. 480-481.
54. Report of the government agent, Kurunegala District, *ibid.*, p. 770.
55. House, *Debates*, Vol. 31, cols. 1938-1940.
56. Tamil Language (Special Provisions) Act, No. 28 of 1958. The text of the act is contained in Appendix III.

language dispute had been resolved. He reported to the SLFP his anxious concern for achieving communal harmony and declared:

I have come to the conclusion that the only principle that should and can be applied is the following: while recognizing the reasonable rights of the majority, the extension of justice and fairplay to the minorities. It is in pursuance of this principle that we have settled the language issue. Sinhalese being the language of 70% of the citizens, it was reasonable that the right of the majority should be conceded in making Sinhalese the only official language of the country. While doing so, it was necessary to extend to our Tamil fellow-citizens the justice of using their language in such matters as education, examinations for the Public Service, correspondence, etc. The language issue can now be considered as settled, and it is not likely that serious communal disturbances will recur in the future.[57]

In September, 1959, Bandaranaike was shot and killed as he greeted a delegation of bhikkhus at his home. Subsequently convicted of conspiring in the assassination was Mapitigama Buddharakkita Thero, a joint secretary and one of the most prominent leaders of the Eksath Bhikkhu Peramuna, an organization which had come to typify extremist incendiarism and the opportunistic manipulation of communal passions.[58] The shock of Bandaranaike's murder added to the stunned amazement of the Ceylonese at the mob fury unleashed in the communal riots. Although the language dispute and communal rivalry soon reappeared, politicians have generally appeared to be less inclined toward impassioned communal incitement without consideration of the possible consequences. The contest between communities since 1958 has been largely contained within the limits of relatively orderly and non-violent competition, whether in Parliament or in the streets. A mas-

57. S. W. R. D. Bandaranaike, "Message by the Prime Minister and Leader of the Party," *Śrī Laṅkā Nidahas Pakṣaya Hatväni Sāṅvatsarika Kalāpaya, 1959* [*Sri Lanka Freedom Party Seventh Annual Number, 1959*] (Colombo: Sri Lanka Freedom Party, 1959), p. 129. Bandaranaike's reference to the proportion of citizens speaking Sinhalese was in error. Sinhalese constitute about 70 per cent of the total population of Ceylon, but 80 per cent of Ceylon citizens.

58. A commission investigating the assassination several years later concluded that, although Buddharakkita's connection with the Eksath Bhikkhu Peramuna was well known and at least two and possibly all three of the persons convicted of murder or conspiracy to murder in Bandaranaike's death were members of Bandaranaike's own SLFP, no organization appeared to be directly involved in the plot. *Report to His Excellency the Governor-General by the Commission Appointed in Terms of the Commissions of Inquiry Act to Inquire into and Report on Certain Matters Connected with the Assassination of the Late Prime Minister Solomon West Ridgeway Dias Bandaranaike* (Sessional Paper III, 1965), p. 11.

sive Tamil *satyagraha* campaign in 1961, although generating intense feelings and producing charges of police and army brutality, was marked by a notable absence of mob violence. A riot connected with the language issue in Colombo early in 1966 quickly subsided after some destruction of property and one death.

CHAPTER V

Coalescence of Tamil opposition

Until the rise to prominence of the official language issue and the election of 1956, G. G. Ponnambalam's Tamil Congress was the most successful political party in the Tamil areas and claimed the right to speak politically for the interests of the community. At the delimitation of parliamentary constituencies preceding the 1947 election, eight of nine Northern Province constituencies and three of seven Eastern Province constituencies contained absolute majorities of Ceylon Tamils, and in one additional constituency in each province (Mannar and Trincomalee) the Ceylon Tamils constituted nearly 50 per cent of the population and formed the largest single ethnic group (see Table 6). Of the thirteen essentially Tamil constituencies, the Tamil Congress won seven in 1947, with most of the others going to independents. In late 1948, Ponnambalam accepted a Cabinet post and the Tamil Congress joined the UNP Government. The Tamil Congress fought the 1952 election in alliance with the UNP and, although only four of its candidates were returned to Parliament, it maintained its position as the most successful single party in the Tamil areas.

At about the time the Tamil Congress had joined the Government in 1948, legislation was enacted defining Ceylonese citizenship to exclude most of the Indian Tamil estate population and depriving them of the franchise they had previously enjoyed. In protest against Tamil Congress acquiescence in the disfranchisement of the Indian Tamils and co-operation with the UNP Government which had drafted the legislation, several of the Tamil Congress M.P.'s led by S. J. V. Chelvanayakam broke away and in 1949 formed a separate political party, called the Federal party or the Ilankai Tamil Arasu Kadchi. The Federal party won only two parliamentary seats in 1952, but in 1956 the language issue abruptly elevated the party to a position of dominance in the Tamil areas. After the sudden UNP reversal of language policy

Table 6. *Northern and Eastern Province constituencies at 1946 delimi-tation: ethnic composition and party affiliation of elected par-liamentary representatives in 1947, 1952, and 1956*

Constituency	Percentage				Party affiliation[a]		
	Ceylon Tamils	Ceylon Moors	Sinhalese	Others	1947	1952	1956
Northern Province							
Kayts	99.2	—	0.2	0.6	Ind	TC	FP
Vaddukkoddai	96.1	—	0.5	3.4	TC	Ind	FP
Kankesanturai	96.4	—	0.7	2.9	TC	UNP	FP
Jaffna	84.2	7.1	2.8	5.9	TC	TC	TC
Kopai	98.1	—	0.2	1.7	TC	FP	FP
Point Pedro	98.3	0.1	0.4	1.2	TC	TC	Com
Chavakachcheri	90.3	0.6	3.7	5.3	TC	TC	FP
Mannar	48.6	29.5	3.5	18.4[b]	Ind	Ind	FP
Vavuniya	66.5	8.2	16.4	7.9	Ind	Ind	Ind
Eastern Province							
Trincomalee	47.8	11.2	22.7	18.3[c]	TC	FP	FP
Mutur	36.5	54.4	3.2	8.9	UNP	Ind	Ind
Kalkudah	52.2	37.8	1.7	8.3	Ind	UNP	Ind
Batticaloa	52.0	28.5	13.0	6.5	UNP	Ind	FP
Paddiruppu	81.2	14.1	1.2	3.5	Ind	Ind	minor
Kalmunai	24.2	67.4	2.5	5.7	UNP	UNP	FP
Pottuvil	25.5	60.0	7.0	7.5	Ind	UNP	FP

[a]Abbreviations: Ind, independent; TC, Tamil Congress; FP, Federal party; UNP, United National Party; Com, Communist party; and minor, minor party.
[b]Includes 10.8 per cent Indian Tamils.
[c]Includes 7.4 per cent Indian Tamils.
Source: Ethnic composition is from *Report of the First Delimitation Commission Appointed in Accordance with Sub-section (I) of Section 76 of the Ceylon (Constitution) Order in Council, 1946* (Sessional Paper XIII, 1946), pp. 72-91. Party affiliations are from Ceylon, Department of Census and Statistics, *Statistical Abstract of Ceylon, 1960* (Colombo: Government Press, 1960), Table 65, pp. 86-88.

and indorsement of Sinhalese-only, the Tamil Congress and the Tamil ex-UNP members, most of whom contested the 1956 election as independents, appeared to be tainted by collaboration with the perfidious UNP. Only the Federal party could claim that it had from the first recognized the communal character of the UNP and the danger to Tamil interests of participation in a Sinhalese-dominated Government. As early as 1948, in his stand against the citizenship act, Chelvanayakam had prophesied the language controversy.[1] As the MEP coalition, pledged to immediate enactment of legislation to make Sinhalese the

1. See Ceylon, House of Representatives, *Parliamentary Debates (Hansard)*, Vol. 5, col. 494.

sole official language, swept to power in the Sinhalese South, the Federal party rode to clear mastery in the Tamil North and East. It captured eight of the thirteen Tamil constituencies and two Eastern Province constituencies with Moor majorities and sizable Tamil minor-

Table 7. *Northern and Eastern Province constituencies at 1959 delimitation: ethnic composition and party affiliation of elected parliamentary representatives in March, 1960; July, 1960; and 1965*

Constituency	Percentage				Party affiliation[a]		
	Ceylon Tamils	Ceylon Moors	Sinhalese	Others	March 1960	July 1960	1965
Northern Province							
Kayts	98.8	0.2	0.6	0.4	FP	FP	FP
Vaddukkoddai	98.6	—	0.8	0.6	FP	FP	FP
Kankesanturai	98.2	—	1.1	0.7	FP	FP	FP
Uduvil	98.6	0.1	0.6	0.7	FP	FP	FP
Jaffna	75.0	11.0	4.0	10.0	Ind	Ind	TC
Nallur	97.2	—	0.8	2.0	FP	FP	FP
Kopai	99.1	—	0.3	0.6	FP	FP	FP
Uduppiddi	98.9	—	0.3	0.8	TC	TC	TC
Point Pedro	98.2	0.1	0.6	1.1	FP	FP	FP
Chavakachcheri	98.7	0.4	0.4	0.5	FP	FP	FP
Kilinochchi	85.8	1.5	6.7	6.0	FP	FP	FP
Mannar	46.0	25.0	5.0	24.0	FP	FP	FP
Vavuniya	67.0	8.0	17.0	8.0	Ind	Ind	TC
Eastern Province							
Trincomalee	50.1	13.7	21.7	14.5	FP	FP	FP
Mutur[b]	33.2	49.0	15.1	2.7			
1st member					FP	FP	FP
2nd member					Ind	SLFP	SLFP
Kalkudah	64.2	30.6	4.2	1.0	FP	FP	UNP
Batticaloa[b]	55.3	36.0	5.2	3.5			
1st member					FP	FP	FP
2nd member					Ind	UNP	UNP
Amparai	6.3	2.0	90.9	0.8	SLFP	SLFP	SLFP
Paddiruppu	95.4	2.8	1.5	0.3	FP	FP	FP
Kalmunai	27.8	68.1	1.9	2.2	minor	FP	Ind
Nintavur	27.6	69.7	1.8	0.9	Ind	Ind	UNP
Pottuvil	35.7	56.0	7.6	0.7	Ind	Ind	Ind

[a]Abbreviations: FP, Federal party; Ind, independent; TC, Tamil Congress; SLFP, Sri Lank Freedom party; UNP, United National party; and minor, minor party.
[b]Two-member constituency.
Source: Ethnic composition is from *Report of the Delimitation Commission* (Sessional Paper XV 1959), pp. 106-135. Party affiliations for the two elections of 1960 are from Ceylon Daily New *Parliaments of Ceylon, 1960* (Colombo: Associated Newspapers of Ceylon, Ltd., [1962]), pp. 100-11 and for the 1965 election from the Colombo newspapers.

ities. The Tamil Congress was reduced to a single member in the 1956 Parliament.

The Federal party maintained its position as spokesman for the Tamil minority during the following decade, in which language and communal issues were at the forefront. A redrawing of constituency boundaries in 1959, which increased the number of elected members of Parliament from 95 to 151, divided the Northern Province into thirteen constituencies, and created five parliamentary seats in the Eastern Province which were likely to be controlled by Tamil votes (see Table 7).[2] In both elections held in 1960, the Federal party won ten of the Northern Province seats and all five of the Tamil seats in the Eastern Province.[3] Five years later, the party repeated its performance in the Northern Province and held onto four of the five Eastern Province Tamil seats. The Tamil Congress appeared to be virtually defunct in 1960. It won only a single seat in each of the elections that year and its leader and central personality, the veteran politician and legislator G. G. Ponnambalam, was defeated twice. By 1965, however, the party was able to make a slight comeback, winning the three Northern Province seats not captured by the Federal party, and Ponnambalam returned to Parliament.

Preservation of the Tamil nation

The Federal party, like the Tamil Congress, was founded as a frankly communal organization intended specifically and solely to protect and promote the interests of the Tamil community. Chelvanayakam told the meeting which launched the party: "We have met together with the common aim of creating an organisation to work for the attainment of freedom for the Tamil speaking people of Ceylon."[4] The party's justification for existence rests on the assumption of the primacy of communal identification and solidarity in politics and the belief that

2. Two two-member constituencies were created in the Eastern Province where Tamils and Moors are intermingled so that it would be possible for each community to elect one of its own members in each of the double constituencies.

3. In addition, in the second election of 1960 the Federal party picked up one Moor seat, but the Moor M.P. resigned from the party the following year.

4. S. J. V. Chelvanayakam, *Presidential Address Delivered at the Inaugural and First Business Meeting of the Ilankai Tamil Arasu Kadchi on 18th December, 1949* (Colombo: Ilankai Tamil Arasu Kadchi, n.d.), p. 1.

the common political interests of all members of the community, by virtue of their ethnic bond, outweigh political interests which internally divide the community. At about the time the Federal party was organized, Chelvanayakam argued that "as long as there are activities directed against communities and as long as those communities are minority communities, they must for their self-protection bind themselves in a communal way."[5]

From its founding, the Federal party avowedly has been devoted to preserving the separate existence of the Tamil community. The entire edifice of Federalist beliefs rests on the conviction that the Ceylon Tamils constitute a separate and distinct nation. The party's first convention in 1951 asserted that

the Tamil-speaking people in Ceylon constitute a nation distinct from that of the Sinhalese by every fundamental test of nationhood, firstly that of a separate historical past in this island at least as ancient and as glorious as that of the Singalese [sic], secondly, by the fact of their being a linguistic entity entirely different from that of the Sinhalese, . . . and finally by reason of their territorial habitation of definite areas which constitute over one-third of this Island.[6]

The claim to nationhood based on a distinctive history, language, and territory has been reiterated by Federal party spokesmen repeatedly. Elaborating on the attributes of Tamil nationhood, the party's president assured a 1961 party convention:

We are a nation by all standards. We inhabit a geographically compact and well-defined territory; we speak a common language; we are proud inheritors of a common heritage and culture as ancient as man himself; and above all, we are bound together by that feeling of oneness which is a necessary ingredient for nationhood, that consciousness which you and I and all of us share whatever the part of the country we may live in.[7]

The election of 1956 simultaneously catapulted the Federal party into leadership of the Tamil community and created what was felt to

5. House, *Debates*, Vol. 5, col. 491. For similar arguments, see A. J. Wilson, "Cultural and Language Rights in the Multi-National Society," *Tamil Culture* (Madras), VII, 1 (Jan., 1958), 22-32.

6. *The Case for a Federal Constitution for Ceylon: Resolutions Passed at the First National Convention of the Ilankai Tamil Arasu Kadchi* (Colombo: Ilankai Tamil Arasu Kadchi, 1951), p. 1.

7. S. M. Rasamanickam, *Presidential Address, Ilankai Tamil Arasu Kadchi 7th Annual Convention, 1961* (Jaffna: Ilankai Tamil Arasu Kadchi, 1961), p. 2.

be the gravest threat the Tamils had faced. Shortly after the election a Federal party convention was convened to formulate the party's strategy and policy following passage of the Sinhalese-only Official Language Act and the heightened communal tensions. A resolution adopted by the convention stated Tamil grievances and proclaimed four demands: (1) the adoption of a federal constitution and the creation of "one or more Tamil linguistic state or states . . . enjoying the widest autonomous and residuary powers consistent with the unity and external security of Ceylon"; (2) bestowal on the Tamil language of "absolute parity of status with Sinhalese as an official language"; (3) amendment of the citizenship laws to grant citizenship on the basis of residency in Ceylon; and (4) "the immediate cessation of colonizing the traditionally Tamil-speaking areas with Sinhalese people."[8] These demands have formed the substance of all subsequent Federal party proposals.

Each of the basic Federalist demands is directly concerned with communal relations and the preservation of the separate existence of the Tamil people. The demand for liberalization of the citizenship laws is intended to allow the Indian Tamils of the interior hill country to acquire citizenship and the franchise, thus increasing the political power of the Tamil-speaking people on the island. Single-minded preoccupation with communal questions has caused the Federal party to ignore almost totally all other questions. A Federalist M.P. once explained that the party's members took little part in debates except on communal and language questions "because we have a special mission, a special mandate, to speak on behalf of the Tamil-speaking people and to give a certain message to this House and to the country."[9] The 1960 Federal party election manifesto declared that the party "concentrates all its attention to achieve freedom for the people whom they [*sic*] represent." All non-communal issues were dismissed with the statement that the party would "support all progressive measures in the economic and social sphere introduced by any government in office."[10]

Concerned with the preservation of the integrity of the Tamil com-

8. The text of the resolution is contained in *Ceylon Faces Crisis* (Colombo: Federal Party, 1957), Appendix I, pp. 29-32.
9. House, *Debates*, Vol. 38, col. 777.
10. *Manifesto of the Ilankai Tamil Arasu Kadchi* (Colombo: Ilankai Tamil Arasu Kadchi, 1960), p. 1.

munity and aware that it is a perpetual minority in Ceylon, the Federalists became convinced that the Tamils would never be safe from
the threat of domination and assimilation by the Sinhalese majority
while the two communities existed together in a unitary state subject
to control by the majority. Chelvanayakam became a determined advocate of Tamil political autonomy as the only way of preserving the
identity of the Tamil community. He explained that without autonomy
"the Tamil people's chances of continuing to exist as a different unit
possessed of their cultures, habits, customs, religions and language will
be lost."[11] The party's ideas on federalism are closely associated with
language, and the Federalists' assumption is that the federating units
will be delimited on the basis of language. At the party's first convention in 1951, the Federalist goal was proclaimed as "the attainment
of freedom for the Tamil-speaking people of Ceylon by the establishment of an autonomous Tamil state on the linguistic basis within the
framework of a Federal Union of Ceylon."[12] A statement of party attitudes on federalism argued for "the creation of two separate linguistic
provinces under the central government with a separate legislature for
each, and these two provincial legislatures to be entrusted with the administration of certain internal affairs relating to education, health, agriculture, industries, law and order and similar subjects."[13]

The Federalists' enthusiasm for federalism is not shared by all
Tamil political leaders. The Tamil Congress leader has deplored the
linking of Tamil language demands with the demand for federalism,
since he believes some accommodation on language is possible but that
federalism is impractical and unattainable as it has aroused the almost
unanimous hostility of the Sinhalese.[14] The Tamil Congress has been
essentially a party of lawyers and public servants who tend to emphasize Tamil career prospects in the South. Thus, Tamil Congress members have seen the language issue principally as a question of discrimination in education and employment. They are less committed than the

11. House, *Debates*, Vol. 24, col. 110.
12. *Case for a Federal Constitution*, p. 9.
13. George Livingstone, *The Tamilians in Ceylon and a Federal Constitution* (Colombo: Ilankai Tamil Arasu Kadchi, n.d.), p. 67.
14. Author's interview with G. G. Ponnambalam, July 18, 1965. See also *Ceylon Daily News*, May 30, 1962, and June 16, 1965; *Ceylon Observer*, May 16, 1965.

Federal party to the development of the Tamil community as a separate and distinct group and are more likely to concede the necessity of a reconciliation with the Sinhalese.

To the Federalists, the adoption of Sinhalese as the sole official language constituted a threat not only to the Tamil language but to the continued separate existence of the Tamil nation. In a public appeal to the Tamil people, the Federal party leader declared that "it is our bounden duty to continue the struggle for the preservation of our language rights lest we disintegrate and lose our national identity."[15] A Federalist M.P. explained Tamil engrossment with the language issue by asserting: "We speak often and repeatedly about language because that is so fundamental to us. Language today is the basis of our culture and our nationality."[16] The party has denounced language disabilities encountered by Tamil public servants and insisted that public service entrance examinations be conducted in Tamil as well as Sinhalese. However, the Federalists seem less concerned with the fate of Tamils employed in the South than with the preservation of Tamil distinctiveness in the North. The party president in 1956 warned: "As a result of the passing of the Sinhala only Act it has become necessary for us to eschew Government Service and find other avenues of employment in the near future. We must make our economy completely independent of employment under Government."[17] Chelvanayakam told the Tamils that "the future of our economy lies in our area only."[18] Federal party members repeatedly have claimed that the language issue is only a symptom of the deeper communal problem and solution of the language dispute would profit the Tamils little, as they would remain exposed to the danger of Sinhalese domination and future threats to their existence. Despite frequent reiteration of Tamil language grievances since 1956, the Federalists have retained a basic conviction that "the Sinhalese-Tamil problem in Ceylon is not a mere matter of language. It is one that affects our very existence as a national entity in this country."[19]

15. The full text of Chelvanayakam's statement is contained in *Ceylon Observer*, May 12, 1962.
16. House, *Debates*, Vol. 39, col. 409.
17. C. Vanniasingam, *Presidential Address, 1956 Annual Convention of the Ilankai Tamil Arasu Kadchi* (Colombo: Ilankai Tamil Arasu Kadchi, 1956), p. 18.
18. *Ceylon Observer*, May 12, 1962.
19. Rasamanickam, *Presidential Address, . . . 1961*, p. 8.

Federalist preoccupation with preserving the Tamil nation has led them to react strongly not only to the language issue but to Sinhalese colonization of predominantly Tamil areas. As the holding of a traditional territory, like the possession of a separate language, is one of the claimed attributes of Tamil nationhood, the Federalists have violently opposed the movement of Sinhalese colonists into territories the Federalists consider Tamil. Since before independence the government has sought to irrigate sparsely populated areas of the island and settle in them landless peasant colonists from the more congested areas.[20] Most of the areas of low population density susceptible to colonization have been in the predominantly Tamil-speaking districts, but colonists have included a large number of Sinhalese since the population pressures have been greatest in the Sinhalese South and West. Between 1946 and 1958, the proportion of Sinhalese in the population of the Eastern Province rose from 7.8 to 11.6 per cent, while the proportion of Ceylon Tamils declined from 46.5 to 40.0 per cent.[21]

To the Federal party, this colonization has appeared to be designed to alter the ethnic composition of the "traditional homeland of the Tamils." It has been seen as part of a plot to create Sinhalese majorities in traditionally Tamil constituencies and thereby destroy what little political power the Tamils possess. Colonization has been considered merely one step in the Sinhalese design to dominate the Tamils and obliterate their separate identity.[22] The creation of a constituency with a Sinhalese majority at the site of the large Gal Oya colonization scheme in the Eastern Province in the 1959 delimitation seemed to confirm the Federalists' fears. One M.P. charged that a similar process was at work in the Trincomalee District of the Eastern Province and demanded:

Can anyone seriously deny that this Government . . . desires to destroy and liquidate the Tamils, destroying their political power? In doing this, the [parliamentary] seats in the Trincomalee District will also go to the Sinhalese and the district will become a Sinhalese majority area. . . . [F]urther Sinhalese colonization in Trincomalee District will result in making the Tamils a minority in their own traditional homeland.[23]

20. A study of the colonization schemes is contained in B. H. Farmer, *Pioneer Peasant Colonization in Ceylon* (London: Oxford University Press, 1957).

21. *Report of the First Delimitation Commission* (Sessional Paper XIII, 1946), p. 84; *Report of the Delimitation Commission* (Sessional Paper XV, 1959), p. 123.

22. E.g., *Ceylon Faces Crisis*, pp. 16-18.

23. House, *Debates*, Vol. 33, col. 1052.

The Federal party and Tamil unity

In its efforts to resist Sinhalese domination, the Federal party has sought to promote the unity and solidarity of the Tamils. The 1960 party manifesto declared that "a truly united and consolidated Tamil-speaking people alone can make their views effective" and claimed that the "Federal Party is the only Party that is working for the unity of the Tamil-speaking people without distinction of caste, creed, or geography."[24] In contrast with Sinhalese society, the factors of class, language, and religion have not been sources of major divisions among the Tamils. The marked divisions of Tamil society are produced by caste and regional differences. The Federal party has repeatedly stressed the need to overcome these cleavages in order to mobilize Tamil strength for the communal contest.

Probably the major obstacle to the unity and solidarity of the Tamil community is the continued importance of caste distinctions. The caste system of the Tamils is considerably more rigid, exclusive, and steeply hierarchical than that of the Sinhalese.[25] In contrast with many areas of India, Brahmins are few in number and have never possessed significant economic or social power. However, in the conservative Hindu Tamil society of Ceylon, the Vellala or cultivator caste has maintained a traditional dominance to the present time.[26] Vellalas have retained control of the land and have virtually monopolized higher education. Among Tamils, the Vellala hold on the professions, higher public service posts, and political leadership is almost complete. Although no means of accurate determination exists, the Vellalas almost certainly constitute a considerably smaller proportion of the Tamil population than the comparable Goyigama caste constitutes in the Sinhalese population. Untouchability and disabilities imposed on lower castes, euphemistically

24. *Manifesto of the Ilankai Tamil Arasu Kadchi*, pp. 10-11.
25. The Sinhalese caste system is free of untouchability, and lingering caste disabilities are few. A large proportion of the population belong to the higher castes. For a study of the Sinhalese caste system, see Bryce Ryan, *Caste in Modern Ceylon* (New Brunswick, N.J.: Rutgers University Press, 1953). Descriptions of the Tamil caste system are contained in James Cartman, *Hinduism in Ceylon* (Colombo: M. D. Gunasena & Co., Ltd., 1957), pp. 132-145; and Michael Banks, "Caste in Jaffna," in E. R. Leach (ed.), *Aspects of Caste in South India, Ceylon and North-West Pakistan*, Cambridge Papers in Social Anthropology No. 2 (London: Cambridge University Press, 1962), pp. 61-77.
26. S. Thillainathan, "Social Pattern in Jaffna," *Ceylon Observer*, June 25, 1962.

called "minority Tamils" or "depressed classes," have persisted in Tamil society and have been the source of some tensions. One report claimed that the "minority Tamils" constituted one-quarter of the entire Tamil population.[27] Caste disabilities among the Tamils have been the subject of frequent taunts and denunciations by Sinhalese opponents of the Federal party. In answer to Federalist charges of Sinhalese oppression, a Sinhalese senator once exclaimed:

> If there is any tyranny imposed on the Tamil people in this country, I make bold to say that it is the tyranny of the *Vellala*. The *Vellala* Tamils will not permit Tamils of the depressed classes to draw a bucket of water from a well or enter a temple. The *Vellala* man is not prepared to concede the fundamental right to his Tamil brother to enter a temple and enjoy freedom of worship and be on a level with him in the act of communing with God.[28]

An organization called the All-Ceylon Minority Tamils' Maha Sabha which emerged to promote the interests of at least some sections of the lower castes has occasionally clashed with the Federal party. The SLFP Government in 1962 apparently was extending patronage to this organization over Federalist protests.[29] A Federal party leader in the same year spoke of efforts to divide the Tamils politically by appealing on caste grounds to the "minority Tamils."[30]

The Federal party has frequently declared its desire to abolish untouchability and reduce caste distinctions in the interest of Tamil unity. The party's first convention in 1951 included in a list of basic aims "the regeneration and unification of the Tamil-speaking people of Ceylon by the removal of all forms of social inequalities and injustices, in particular that of untouchability wherever it exists."[31] The Federalist president a few years later urged intensified efforts to eliminate untouchability, declaring: "The Tamil speaking people as a whole should be reassured that the establishment of Tamil Arasu [state] is not for the benefit of any section of the Tamil speaking people but for all of them."[32]

Despite accusations that as the Federal party activists are almost en-

27. Ananda Dassanayake, "The Shame of Jaffna," *Ceylon Observer*, June 12, 1962.
28. Ceylon, Senate, *Parliamentary Debates (Hansard)*, Vol. 10, cols. 693-694.
29. See House, *Debates*, Vol. 46, cols. 1087-1089, 1095-1096.
30. S. M. Rasamanickam, *The Presidential Address at the National Convention of the Ilankai Tamil Arasu Kadchi, 1962* (Colombo: Ilankai Tamil Arasu Kadchi, 1962), p. 9.
31. *Case for a Federal Constitution*, p. 9.
32. Vanniasingam, *Presidential Address, 1956*, p. 19.

tirely from the higher castes the party is not seriously intent on disturbing caste practices, there are indications that the party has attempted to
take action to alleviate some of the more obvious low-caste disabilities.
The party's president in 1956 claimed that a "temple entry committee"
had secured the admittance of untouchables to several temples in Jaffna
and that all temples in the Batticaloa District had recently been opened
to all Hindus without regard to caste.[33] His successor as president mentioned the formation of an "action committee" to work for the removal
of caste disabilities following a conference on the problem convened
by the party in Jaffna.[34] The recent election of a low-caste Tamil to the
Senate by the party's parliamentary delegation was cited by Chelvanayakam as an act which would give status to the low-caste people and
heighten their sense of involvement and participation in the community's political struggles.[35]

Regional differences have separated the Tamils of the Eastern Province and the Tamils of Jaffna in the North, much as divisions have existed between the Kandyan and Low-Country Sinhalese. The Eastern
Province is sparsely populated, with Tamils and Moors living intermingled or in local concentrations, in contrast with the dense, compact
Tamil population of the Jaffna Peninsula. The Jaffna Tamils have enjoyed superior educational and occupational opportunities, and political
as well as business, professional, and intellectual leadership within the
Tamil community has come primarily from Jaffna.

In more than two decades, the Tamil Congress made little effort to
extend its activities to the Eastern Province, preferring to concentrate
on the more accessible and politically conscious North. In contrast, the
Federal party, anxious to maximize Tamil strength and unity, made
early and determined efforts to mobilize support from the east-coast
Tamils. The party, however, is commonly said to have continued to be
controlled from Jaffna. Suggestions of resentment over the Jaffna preponderance in the party have occasionally appeared.[36] Perhaps to mini-

33. *Ibid.*
34. Rasamanickam, *Presidential Address . . . , 1962*, p. 9.
35. Interview by the author, July 2, 1965. Half the members of the thirty-member
Senate are chosen by the House of Representatives by a system of proportional representation which allows every party of significant size to elect one or more of its members.
36. For example, a party official in the Eastern Province issued a sharp public denunciation of the Jaffna politicians for planning party activities without consulting
party members in the East. *Ceylon Observer,* June 5, 1962. Similarly, see *Times of
Ceylon,* Sept. 20, 1962.

mize such resentment, the third and fourth presidents of the party were from the Eastern Province.[37] While acknowledging some differences in interests and outlook between Tamils of the Eastern and Northern Provinces, Federalists claim that in present circumstances the differences are not politically significant. On the compelling questions of the official language and feared Sinhalese domination, there has been no indication of dissension between Tamils of the two regions. The election results over the past decade suggest that, as the Federalists claim, the party has succeeded in attracting the support of most Eastern Province Tamils.

Relations with other Tamil-speaking communities

Tamil is the language of the Ceylon Moors, as well as the Tamils. About one-third of the Ceylon Moors live in the Eastern Province intermingled with Tamils, another third live on the west coast from Kalutara to Mannar, and the remainder are scattered throughout the island.[38] The Moors have been divided on the language issue by area of residence. For the most part, those living in the Sinhalese areas of the island have acquiesced in Sinhalese as the sole official language. The two principal organizations of the community, led by wealthy merchants of the Southwest, announced their willingness to accept a Sinhalese-only language policy.[39] The Federal party has attempted to win the support of the Eastern Province Moors, but with modest success at most. In 1956, Federalist Moors won two of the three Eastern Province constituencies with Moor majorities, but both later deserted the Federal party and joined the Government. The only Moor elected as a Federal party candidate in July, 1960, resigned from the party the following year. In 1965, one Moor was successful as a Federal party candidate, but in a two-member constituency with a substantial Tamil population.

The Moors of the Eastern Province are an agricultural people who

37. S. J. V. Chelvanayakam was the party's first president. He was succeeded by C. Vanniasingham, N. R. Rajavarothiam, and S. M. Rasamanickam. In 1964, Chelvanayakam again assumed the office. In the dozen years he was not the formal head of the party, Chelvanayakam continued to be recognized as its principal leader.

38. Ceylon, Department of Census and Statistics, *Census of Ceylon, 1953*, I (Colombo: Government Press, 1957), 182-183.

39. See I. D. S. Weerawardana, *Ceylon General Election, 1956* (Colombo: M. D. Gunasena & Co., Ltd., 1960), pp. 193-195; Senate, *Debates*, Vol. 10, cols. 448-451.

have experienced slight economic or educational advance in modern times. Their political leaders seem to depend on traditional status and patronage, rather than party organization or declared positions on issues of public policy, for electoral success and once elected are relatively free of party or constituency constraints. Many are elected as independents and others switch party labels with ease. Whatever the scarcely articulated official language sentiments of the Eastern Province Moors may be, a number of their political leaders have been able to accommodate themselves to Governments pledged to Sinhalese-only.

Although often sympathetic with the Federal party language stand, leaders of the east-coast Moors are conscious of the obvious control of the Federal party by Tamils and are strongly aware of their separate ethnic identity. As one leading Moor politician asserted, "this country is the home not merely of the Tamils and Sinhalese but also of a third nation, the Ceylon Moors."[40] The bond of a common language has seldom proved strong enough to overcome consciousness of the ethnic and religious separation and divergent political outlook. By 1965, the Federalists seemed to concede that their party commanded slight support from the Eastern Province Moors.[41]

The Indian Tamils of the interior hill country, who are predominantly estate laborers, are a sizable community of Tamil-speaking people, slightly outnumbering the Ceylon Tamils. Relations between the two Tamil-speaking communities, however, have not been particularly close. The Indian Tamils have tended to remain isolated on the estates, where they commonly live in "coolie lines" tightly bound by networks of caste and kinship.[42] They have generally adhered closely to political or labor organizations and leadership of their own community. Most of the estate laborers are of very low caste and are near the bottom of the socio-economic scale in Ceylon. Many Ceylon Tamils admit misgivings about establishing connections with the Indian Tamils. Language and religion are common to the two communities, but differences of historical background, economic position and occupation, caste, and intangible factors of identification have militated against a close unity.

40. House, *Debates*, Vol. 30, col. 1508.
41. Conversations with Federal party leaders.
42. On the social organization of the estate population, see R. Jayaraman, "Caste and Kinship in a Ceylon Tea Estate," *Economic Weekly* (Bombay), XVI, 8 (Feb. 22, 1964), 393-397.

The Indian Tamils have been a significant element in the island's population for only about a century.[43] For many decades the estate laborers coming to Ceylon left their families in India and returned to India when employment slackened. Although most Indian Tamils today were born in Ceylon and in recent times members of the community have lost their ties with India, they are still widely viewed as alien interlopers without a permanent interest in the island, as is implied by the persistent reference to them as "Indians" or "Indian" Tamils.[44] It was on the basis of their lack of indigenous roots and abiding interest in Ceylon that they were largely excluded from Ceylonese citizenship after independence. Subject to residence requirements, the Indian Tamils as British subjects were entitled to vote in Ceylon before independence. A doubling of the number of legislative constituencies in 1947 created much smaller electorates than existed previously, with the result that local concentrations of Indian Tamils could more often decide or influence elections. Also, an increasing proportion of the Indian Tamils were beginning to exercise their right to vote by 1947. Seven members of their communal party, the Ceylon Indian Congress founded in 1939, were elected to the first Parliament in 1947.[45] In constituencies in which the Indian Tamils were a minority, their votes were believed to have gone heavily to the Marxist parties.[46] Consequently, at independence, which followed soon after the 1947 election, the political strength of the Indian Tamils seemed to be growing and to be opposed to the UNP and allied politicians attempting to create a stable parliamentary majority. Sinhalese popular apprehension concerning political influence obtained by the "alien" Indian Tamils may have been reinforced by the desire of the politicians in power to capture the constituencies won in 1947 by the Ceylon Indian Congress and remove an important source of support for their Marxist opponents.[47] Statutes adopted in 1948 and 1949 de-

43. A good summary of the history and position of the Indian Tamils in Ceylon is contained in W. Howard Wriggins, *Ceylon: Dilemmas of a New Nation* (Princeton: Princeton University Press, 1960), pp. 212-228.

44. Federal party spokesmen object to the "Indian" label for these people and commonly refer to them as "hill-country" or "estate" Tamils.

45. One was elected as an independent and subsequently joined the Ceylon Indian Congress.

46. It was estimated that Indian Tamil votes were decisive in the election of twelve to fourteen Marxist candidates. Sir W. Ivor Jennings, *The Constitution of Ceylon* (3rd ed.; London: Oxford University Press, 1953), p. 29.

47. The political considerations leading to and the political consequences of the dis-

fined Ceylonese citizenship to exclude most of the Indian Tamils and restricted the suffrage to citizens of Ceylon.

Since the Indian Tamil disfranchisement, the Ceylon Indian Congress (renamed the Ceylon Democratic Congress to avoid the alien and communal connotations of the original name) has continued to contest a few parliamentary constituencies, but has not succeeded in electing a single candidate to Parliament. The 134,000 Indian Tamils who have obtained Ceylonese citizenship have constituted only a marginal electoral influence in a few constituencies in the estate areas of the interior highlands. The Indian Tamils, possessing only a feeble voice in the constitutional political process, have remained generally quiescent politically. The interests of the community have been championed in the political arena at times by the (largely Sinhalese) Marxist parties and by estate workers' trade unions. The principal organization of the Indian Tamil estate workers is the Ceylon Workers' Congress (CWC), an outgrowth of the Ceylon Indian Congress, which with 350,000 members is the largest labor organization in Ceylon. The CWC sponsored a 100-day *satyagraha* campaign in 1952 protesting the political disabilities of the Indian Tamils and more recently has vigorously denounced provisions of the 1964 agreement between India and Ceylon for the repatriation to India of more than half a million Indian Tamils.[48]

A split in the CWC in 1956, interrupted by a brief reconciliation in 1960-1961, produced a second large trade union essentially limited to Indian Tamil estate workers, the Democratic Workers' Congress (DWC). Like the CWC, the DWC has been preoccupied with the problems of the Indian Tamil community resulting from the denial to them of Ceylonese citizenship.[49] The two organizations, however, have frequently taken conflicting political positions. In the 1965 election, for example, the CWC indorsed the UNP while the DWC supported a rival coalition composed of the SLFP, LSSP, and Communist party.

---

franchisement of the Indian Tamils are discussed in I. D. S. Weerawardana, "Minority Problems in Ceylon," *Pacific Affairs*, XXV, 3 (Sept., 1952), 278-287. Also, see Sir W. Ivor Jennings, "Politics in Ceylon," *Far Eastern Survey*, XXI, 17 (Dec. 3, 1952), 177-180.

48. *Ceylon Workers' Congress Report, 1964-1965* (Colombo: Ceylon Workers' Congress, n.d.), pp. 2, 41-44, 61-63.

49. E.g., *Presidential Address of Mr. A. Aziz at the Annual Sessions of the Democratic Workers' Congress Held at Yatiyantota on the 17th of August, 1963* (Colombo: Democratic Workers' Congress, n.d.), pp. 2-5.

The Federal party leaders look on the Indian Tamils as natural allies in their fight to preserve the Tamil language and resist the power of the Sinhalese majority. The Federalists often point out that their party was formed after a split in the Tamil Congress precipitated by the denial of citizenship to the Indian Tamils. Addressing the first meeting of the Federal party, Chelvanayakam spoke of the Indian Tamil estate laborers and urged that the Ceylon Tamils "make these people's case their own."[50] The party has regularly included among its basic demands a call for revision of the citizenship laws in favor of the Indian Tamils. Until about 1961 the Federal party and the CWC had made some gestures toward mutual co-operation. In April, 1961, the CWC staged a one-day token strike as an expression of support for a *satyagraha* campaign being conducted in the North and East by the Federalists. The reopening of the division between the CWC and DWC in 1961 removed from the CWC the leadership element most inclined toward close co-operation with the Federalists. This development, perhaps accompanied by apprehension of rivalry in leading the Tamil-speaking peoples of Ceylon, was followed by an abrupt deterioration of relations between the CWC and the Federal party, with CWC leaders publicly disclaiming any sympathy with Federalist policies and denouncing Federalist efforts to champion the cause of the estate workers.[51]

As the rupture with the CWC developed, the Federal party commenced direct approaches to the Indian Tamils. In opposing a bill to Ceylonize estate labor in 1962, Chelvanayakam declared his party to be "the only national organization which seeks to represent the entire Tamil-speaking people of this country—the hill country Tamils, the Muslim people and all other Tamils resident in the rest of the country."[52] A short time later plans were announced to establish Federal party branch organizations in the hill country among the Indian Tamils.[53] At the end of 1962 the Federal party formed a trade union for estate workers, the Ilankai Thollilalar Kazham, as a demonstration of the party's solidarity with the estate Tamils. The Indian Tamil estate workers seem to be primarily concerned with labor questions, and

50. Chelvanayakam, *Presidential Address* . . . , *1949*, p. 15.
51. E.g., see *Ceylon Observer*, April 30, 1962; *Ceylon Daily News*, June 7, 1962, and June 13, 1962; *Times of Ceylon*, June 29, 1962.
52. *Ceylon Daily News*, June 5, 1962.
53. Rasamanickam, *Presidential Address* . . . , *1962*, p. 10.

trade unions are the only organizations which have had much success among them. Although considerable Federalist attention and energy have been devoted to creating ties with the Indian Tamils in recent years, little indication has yet appeared that the efforts are achieving significant results.

Federal party tactics

The tasks assumed by the Federal party have been recognized as formidable undertakings for a party representing a minority community. However, the Federalists, who often compare themselves to Parnell's Irish Nationalists, have believed that unrelenting agitation and obstruction backed by a united and determined Tamil community eventually could force concessions from a Sinhalese-dominated government. Like most Ceylonese parties, the Federal party was organized and continues to be dominated by members of Parliament. It is probable that the Federalists' initial expectation was to seek their goals chiefly in the parliamentary arena. However, the widening political rift between communities following the Sinhalese-only movement and the helplessness of Tamil parliamentary representatives at the adoption of the Official Language Act apparently prompted the Federalists to emphasize extra-parliamentary methods of struggle. The party organized a hartal in the North and East in February, 1956, and as the language bill was debated in Parliament, a Federalist-sponsored demonstration was conducted near the Parliament building. The following August, a party convention accepted the Gandhian technique of *satyagraha* or non-violent resistence in its struggle with the government as, in Chelvanayakam's words, "a recognized political weapon in the hands of a weaker people against hard-hearted rulers."[54] The convention adjourned with the threat that unless steps were taken to create a federal state within one year, the party would "launch direct action by non-violent means for the achievement of this objective."[55] The threatened *satyagraha* was canceled as a result of the mid-1957 agreement contained in the Bandaranaike-Chelvanayakam Pact. After the collapse of the accord in 1958, the eruption of communal riots and political confusion the fol-

54. House, *Debates*, Vol. 33, col. 1034.
55. *Ceylon Faces Crisis*, p. 32.

lowing year created by the breakup of the MEP coalition in May and
the assassination of Bandaranaike in September postponed a renewal
of concerted Federalist efforts until 1960.

An election in March, 1960, provided the Federalists with an opportunity they had long been seeking. As the representatives of a perpetual minority, they could never hope to win a majority in Parliament.
Yet, the Federalists harbored the hope that their small but monolithic
band might at some opportune moment hold the balance between rival
Sinhalese parties in the often closely divided Parliament. They would
then be in a position to bargain for the attainment of Tamil aims. Chelvanayakam warned the Federalists at the first meeting of the party that
the Tamils had been betrayed in the past by leaders who compromised
Tamil interests in exchange for office and argued that "like the Irish
Nationalists" they must remain dedicated and avoid compromise or
the lure of office until their goal was won.[56] In the deadlocked Parliament after March, 1960, a Government was formed by the UNP as
the largest single party, but with fifty seats the UNP parliamentary
group fell short of a minimum majority. As there was no prospect that
the SLFP or the Marxists would support the UNP, the votes of the
fifteen Federal party members were essential for the UNP Government to survive. On the other hand, for the SLFP to bring the UNP
Government down or form an alternative Government, it, too, needed
the co-operation of the Federal party. It seemed that favorable parliamentary circumstances might gain for the Tamils the accommoda-
tions they were seeking.

At the request of UNP Prime Minister Dudley Senanayake, the
Federalists prepared a list of their party's minimum conditions for extending parliamentary support to the Government. The conditions included recognition of the Tamil language as "a national language of
the Tamil-speaking people in Ceylon" and acceptance of Tamil as the
"language of administration and of the courts of law" in the Northern
and Eastern Provinces. Also included were demands for the creation
of autonomous regional bodies with powers over colonization and other
matters and the liberalization of the citizenship laws to the advantage
of the Indian Tamils.[57] The conditions were rejected by the UNP as

56. Chelvanayakam, *Presidential Address* . . . , *1949*, pp. 8, 14.
57. The statement of conditions is quoted in House, *Debates*, Vol. 38, cols. 780-785.

closely paralleling the provisions of the Bandaranaike-Chelvanayakam Pact which the UNP had strenuously opposed.[58] With the Federal party in opposition, the UNP Government lost its first test in Parliament. The developments led Chelvanayakam to observe:

> One important lesson that the present situation ought to teach us is that no party could afford to ignore—much less to offend—the feelings of a minority community when the party frames and propagates its policies. The U.N.P. did not imagine that the situation would arise when it would require Tamil support to enable it to remain in power.[59]

The Federalist leader joined with leaders of the SLFP and several other parties in issuing a statement declaring their readiness to support a Government organized by the SLFP.[60] However, instead of appointing an alternative Government, the governor-general dissolved Parliament and called a new election.

The election which followed in July produced an SLFP majority in Parliament, and the widow of S. W. R. D. Bandaranaike, Sirimavo Bandaranaike, became prime minister. The initial optimism of the Federalists over the election results quickly evaporated as the new Government pledged a rapid shift to Sinhalese as the sole language of administration. The Federalists believed themselves betrayed. According to Chelvanayakam, when negotiations with the UNP failed, he began talks with the leaders of the SLFP on the basis of the same statement given to the UNP. The SLFP representatives rejected the requested changes in the citizenship laws and suggested minor alterations of other conditions. On the critical language issue, Chelvanayakam related, they implied agreement and indicated that the Federal party demands were similar to their own intentions. After Federalist co-operation in overturning the UNP Government led to the July election and the SLFP victory, the Federal party leader attempted to persuade the Government to honor the understanding but, Chelvanayakam charged, the SLFP Government was "clearly carrying on an unadulterated 'Sinhala only' policy without being conscious of any moral obligation that they owe us."[61] A minister who had been a representative of the SLFP

58. See Dudley Senanayake's statement, *ibid.*, Vol. 45, col. 1918.
59. *Ibid.*, Vol. 38, col. 205.
60. *Ceylon Observer*, April 24, 1960.
61. House, *Debates*, Vol. 45, cols. 1802-1817.

at the talks conceded the substance of Chelvanayakam's statement, but
claimed there was no firm commitment and he and his colleagues had
merely stated SLFP intentions.[62] The Federal party had lost the opportunity to secure its objectives by parliamentary maneuver. The dissolution of Parliament in April, the SLFP majority in July which freed
the SLFP from continued dependence on the Federal party, and the
subsequent disinterest of the SLFP Government in granting any of the
Federalist claims combined to rob the Federal party of any gain from
its pivotal position after the March election.

Unable to make any progress toward a language settlement more
than four years after the passage of the Official Language Act and con-
fronted by an increasingly rigorous implementation of the Sinhalese-
only legislation, the Federalists resolved to protest the language developments by using their last weapon, a full-scale *satyagraha* and civil
disobedience movement in the Tamil areas. The party had held in re-
serve the threat of a *satyagraha* campaign since 1956. As the population
in the North and much of the East was almost entirely Tamil-speaking
and the public servants in these areas were mostly Tamils, the Federalists believed the Government could not control a movement of total
opposition in the Tamil areas and rather than display its impotence it
would negotiate with the Tamil leaders. A militant direct-action campaign was also calculated to demonstrate Tamil solidarity and determination to the Government.

The *satyagraha* was launched in Jaffna on February 20, 1961, and
spread to Batticaloa, Trincomalee, Mannar, and Vavuniya. *Satyagrahis*
sat and squatted before the *kachcheris* housing the district offices of the
central government. By blocking entrance to the offices and appealing to
Tamil public servants, the *satyagrahis* brought governmental activity to
a virtual standstill throughout the Tamil areas. Rations of state-sub-
sidized rice were not distributed and wage and pension payments were
suspended in an attempt, according to the Federalists, to bring economic
pressure to bear against the Tamil population.[63] In March, army and
navy units were dispatched to the North and East. Talks were held between the minister of justice and the Federalist leadership, but resulted

62. *Ibid.*, Vol. 45, cols. 1817-1839.
63. Rasamanickam, *Presidential Address* . . . , *1962*, pp. 3-5.

in Government rejection of the Federal party conditions for ending the campaign.

Frustrated at the stalemate as the campaign advanced into its second month, the Federalists resolved on an act of civil disobedience in an attempt to force the Government to take repressive action against them. In defiance of the postal laws, they established a postal service and issued their own stamps. The Government at once proclaimed a state of emergency, ordered the arrest of the Federalist leaders, and proscribed the Federal party. In announcing the measures, Mrs. Bandaranaike charged that "the Federal leaders have challenged the lawfully established Government of this country with a view to establishing a separate State."[64] With the Government action, the campaign was abandoned after an extensive disruption of civil administration lasting more than two months. The Federal party leaders were held in custody until October, and the emergency remained in force for two years. The *satyagraha*, considered by many to be the Tamils' strongest weapon, had been played out and had obtained no relaxation of official language policy. The Federalists could claim only that the *satyagraha* conclusively demonstrated "that all the Tamil speaking people of the country were united in the defence of their language rights and in their opposition to the Government's discriminatory policies."[65]

After the Tamil areas had returned to normal and the Federalists were released from custody following the *satyagraha*, opposition to implementation of the Sinhalese-only legislation was quickly resumed. In May, 1962, Chelvanayakam urged obstruction and non-co-operation, pleading for Tamil public servants and students to refuse to study the Sinhalese language.[66] Tamil grievances and demands were reiterated in Parliament and the press. However, the Tamils seemed exhausted after the termination of the *satyagraha*, and their leaders appeared to be waiting for a change of circumstances that would provide them with a fresh opportunity to pursue their goals.

Since the Sinhalese-only storm had arisen, the Federal party had at-

64. *Ceylon News*, April 27, 1961. The Federalists repeatedly have denied that their act had a separatist objective. E.g., Rasamanickam, *Presidential Address* . . . , *1962*, p. 4; Senate, *Debates*, Vol. 17, cols. 2404-2405; House, *Debates*, Vol. 46, col. 2151.
65. S. J. V. Chelvanayakam, *Presidential Address, Ilankai Tamil Arasu Kadchi Ninth National Convention, 1964* (Colombo: Ilankai Tamil Arasu Kadchi, 1964), p. 10.
66. *Ceylon Observer*, May 12, 1962.

tempted threats of direct action, use of its position of balance in Parliament, and eventually resort to direct action in attempts to win modification of the official language policy. The party discovered, however, progressively greater rigidity in Sinhalese attitudes on the language question. Frustration and helplessness before the political strength of the Sinhalese majority bred progressive Tamil alienation. In 1962, a Federalist M.P. charged: "This imperialist Government is establishing a colonial state in our part of the country."[67] Another asserted two years later: "The Sinhala only policy of this Government means not merely the elimination of the Tamil language from its due place in the public life of this country but the shutting out of the Tamil-speaking people of this country from the political, economic and cultural life of Ceylon."[68] It was nine years after passage of the Official Language Act when, following the 1965 election, political circumstances made it possible for the Tamils to realize at least their minimum language demands. Bitter conflict among the predominantly Sinhalese parties, momentarily overshadowing the communal rivalry, and the failure of any single party to win a parliamentary majority, again making Tamil support crucial for the formation of a Government, provided the setting for the first official steps toward accommodating Tamil language interests since the rise of the Sinhalese-only movement.[69]

Separatist and pan-Dravidian sentiment

The unabating communal conflict after 1956 created the potential for a growth of separatist sentiment among the Tamils, and many Sinhalese have been apprehensive that the real Tamil political objective is separation. One prominent Tamil politician has openly championed separatism, to be achieved by violence if necessary. C. Suntharalingam, who as an independent member of Parliament served in the first post-independence Cabinet, wrote bluntly: "Today circumstances . . . compel the ancient proud Thamil nation inhabiting this land from time immemorial to have their traditional homelands constituted and converted into a separate and distinct nation-state by peaceful methods if possible,

67. House, *Debates*, Vol. 46, col. 1761.
68. *Ibid.*, Vol. 56, col. 247.
69. See chap. vi.

by other methods, if necessary."[70] Since taking up the cause of separation, however, Suntharalingam does not appear to have enjoyed a strong political following. He resigned from Parliament in 1959 and was defeated in three subsequent attempts to return.

Federal party demands for autonomy and emphasis on the distinctiveness of the Tamil nation have been interpreted by some as tantamount to separatism. The party's Tamil name, Ilankai Tamil Arasu Kadchi, the approximate translation of which is Ceylon Tamil State party, has been claimed to imply a separatist goal, as the word *arasu* is said to connote an independent sovereign state rather than a component of a federal state.[71] The Federalists, however, have regularly restated their objective as autonomy within a federal union rather than total political separation. The Federal party's 1960 election manifesto, disclaiming aspirations for a separate Tamil state as "suicidal to the interests of the people of Ceylon as a whole," described the party's objective as "a reasonable share of the governmental power for the Tamil-speaking people in their traditional homelands and even here in respect of subjects which are of local importance."[72]

With the failure of a language settlement to materialize years after the passage of the Official Language Act, mounting frustration prompted warnings of separatism by Tamil leaders. Ponnambalam in 1958 argued that imposition of the Sinhalese language would drive the Tamils to seek separation.[73] While denying that the Federal party sought an independent state, the party's president in 1961 noted that "there are large and influential sections of the Tamil people who now think on those lines."[74] An ominous note of warning appeared in a statement in Parliament by the Federal party secretary in 1964:

I think every year the development of events in the South leads us to the irresistible conclusion that the hopes of union are receding further and further. If the leaders of the Sinhalese people persist in this attitude, I will say, when

70. C. Suntharalingam, "Eelam: Our Deity," a leaflet dated December 18, 1959, published by the author in Jaffna. Curiously, Suntharalingam, then a university mathematics professor, was credited with devising the scheme by which the "pan-Sinhalese ministry" was formed in 1936.

71. E.g., D. C. Vijayavardhana, *The Revolt in the Temple* (Colombo: Sinha Publications, 1953), pp. 445-448. Also, see Weerawardana, *Ceylon General Elections, 1956*, pp. 186-188.

72. *Manifesto of the Ilankai Tamil Arasu Kadchi*, p. 5.

73. House, *Debates*, Vol. 31, col. 163.

74. Rasamanickam, *Presidential Address, . . . 1961*, p. 8.

you will be advocating federalism, we will rather choose to have a division of this country even at the cost of several lives. . . . We will rather have a division of this country than surrender as a nation without self-respect and be eternal slaves in this country.[75]

The prospect of Tamil separatism is viewed with particular apprehension by many Sinhalese because of the dread of Ceylon Tamil association in a pan-Dravidian movement from South India, which might not only destroy the political unity of Ceylon but introduce into the island the power of the many millions of Dravidian-speaking peoples in India. Sinhalese fear of the large Dravidian-speaking population in nearby South India was expressed by a prominent Sinhalese politician, who contended: "In this country the problem of the Tamils is not a minority problem. The Sinhalese are the minority in Dravidastan. We are carrying on a struggle for our national existence against the Dravidastan majority."[76] Contacts between Ceylon Tamils and the Dravida Munnetra Kazhagam (DMK) in Madras, which until recently openly advocated an independent Dravidian or Tamil state in South India, are watched with particular suspicion by many Sinhalese. Sirimavo Bandaranaike, shortly after she ceased to be prime minister, wrote that the DMK objective was to establish an independent Tamil state with the aid of the Dravidian-speaking peoples of India, Ceylon, and Malaya, and charged that a close connection existed between the DMK and the leaders of the Federal party.[77]

By 1962 an organization calling itself the Dravida Munnetra Kazhagam of Ceylon had appeared among the Indian Tamil estate workers.[78] It is said to have been inspired by the DMK of Madras but to have no organizational ties outside the island. It does not appear to have gained much strength before it was banned by the government in 1962. The Federal party, then itself beginning efforts to establish contacts with the Tamil-speaking estate laborers, reported some co-operation in the hill country with the Ceylon DMK and denounced the banning of the organization.[79] The Ceylon DMK intervened in the dispute be-

75. House, *Debates*, Vol. 56, cols. 255-256.
76. *Ibid.*, Vol. 48, col. 1313.
77. Sirimavo Dias Bandaranaike, *Sinhalayāgē Anāgataya hā Indu Laṅkā Praśnaya* [*The Future of the Sinhalese and the Indo-Ceylon Question*] (Colombo: Jātika Adhyāpana Maṇḍalaya, 1965), p. 41.
78. See *Ceylon Observer*, June 19, 1962, and June 25, 1962.
79. Rasamanickam, *Presidential Address . . .*, *1962*, p. 9.

tween the Federal party and the Ceylon Workers' Congress by issuing a statement defending the Federalists against CWC denunciations and lauding their efforts on behalf of the Indian Tamils.[80]

The parallel between South Indian fear of North Indian Aryan domination and Ceylon Tamil fear of Sinhalese domination has not escaped the notice of the Ceylon Tamils. A few goodwill messages and visits have been exchanged between the Ceylonese and South Indian Tamil politicians. Early in 1965, amid violent anti-Hindi agitation in Madras, Chelvanayakam on behalf of the Federal party sent a message to the general secretary of the DMK in Madras proclaiming an "identity between your great struggle [against Hindi] and the resistance [to Sinhalese] we are putting up here in Ceylon."[81] Nonetheless, little if any sentiment for coalescence in a greater Tamilnad or Dravidastan or interest in foreign Dravidian-based political movements appears to exist among Ceylon Tamil leaders. One Federalist spokesman replied to accusations of links between the Federal party and the DMK by insisting that "we have no relationship whatsoever, no connection whatsoever, with the D.M.K. of South India."[82] Another reassured the Sinhalese: "You sometimes suspect that we may join South India. That has never been our intention. I would like to say that we want to live as one with the Sinhala people in a united Ceylon."[83] Even the fiery Suntharalingam explicitly disassociated his proposals for an independent Ceylon Tamil state from any connection with a pan-Tamil movement or the DMK.[84] Ceylon Tamils point to the considerably higher standard of living in Ceylon, the weakness of sentimental bonds between Tamils of Ceylon and India, and the long-standing Ceylon Tamil identification with the island as inhibiting Ceylonese interest in pan-Dravidianism. Despite a few contacts and mutual assurances of good will between Tamil politicians of Ceylon and India, only a further marked deterioration of communal relations or greatly increased frustration with the situation in Ceylon seems likely to impel the Ceylon Tamils toward serious involvement in a pan-Dravidian movement.

80. *Ceylon Daily News*, June 11, 1962.
81. *Ibid.*, Feb. 17, 1965.
82. Senate, *Debates*, Vol. 22, col. 651.
83. House, *Debates*, Vol. 48, col. 772.
84. *Ibid.*, Vol. 33, cols. 1165-1166.

CHAPTER VI

Partisan competition and the language issue

The pattern of partisan competition in championing Sinhalese language aspirations which emerged before the 1956 election continued to reappear throughout the following decade. The 1956 election had confirmed the feasibility of obtaining governmental power by exclusive reliance on the votes of the Sinhalese majority. Although political parties had previously experienced slight success in attracting both Sinhalese and Tamil voters, the official language issue produced an almost total partisan cleavage between communities. Electoral competition seemed to require that parties contending for Sinhalese support declare their enthusiastic and uncompromising dedication to Sinhalese language aspirations, effectively precluding them from simultaneous appeals for Tamil support. In the three elections between the mid-fifties and the election of 1965, the Sri Lanka Freedom party and the United National party, the two principal competitors for power, did not contest a single Tamil constituency. To Tamil spokesmen, hope for the recognition of minority interests and resolution of the language dispute seemed futile as long as the language question remained "an election issue between the rival political parties that contest only the areas of the Sinhalese speaking people."[1] Partisan appeals to Sinhalese language and communal sentiments impeded the reconciliation of conflicting Sinhalese and Tamil claims, and partisan rivalry helped maintain the official language issue as a major source of political conflict and controversy.

The UNP and communal issues

After the United National party's shattering defeat in the 1956 election, a concerted effort was begun to revamp the party and bring it

1. Ceylon, House of Representatives, *Parliamentary Debates (Hansard)*, Vol. 38, col. 643.

into harmony with the political currents revealed by the election. Sir John Kotelawala was persuaded to retire, and party leadership was conferred on Dudley Senanayake, the widely respected former prime minister and son of D. S. Senanayake. Dudley Senanayake believed the gravest error of the UNP prior to 1956 was its failure to appreciate the power of appeals to language and religious sentiments.[2] He presided over the drafting of a new party program, adopted by a party conference in March, 1958, which was intended to reflect the UNP's new popular and progressive orientation, including a sharpened concern with Sinhalese linguistic, religious, and cultural aspirations. On the language issue, the program emphasized that the party remained committed to the Sinhalese-only position it assumed in February, 1956. Within the Sinhalese-only framework, statutory provisions for the use of Tamil in education, public service examinations, parliamentary proceedings, and public contacts with the government were promised.[3] This statement has continued as the basis of UNP policy on the official language.

After 1956, the UNP found itself with little room to maneuver on the language question, as the party's devotion to Sinhalese language and communal aspirations was suspect. The constraints of electoral pressure from the Sinhalese majority were suggested in one UNP spokesman's explanation of his party's failure to reach agreement with the Federal party in 1960:

If we agree to their proposals I can straightaway say that we can never go back to the country in another election. We will be hounded out if we say that we have agreed to the requirements of the Federal Party. I am perfectly certain that the same fate will come to the S.L.F.P. if they happen to go to the polls in the near future. They will not be able to face the polls.[4]

The Bandaranaike-Chelvanayakam Pact provided the UNP with an opportunity to appear as the champion of Sinhalese interests in competition with the Bandaranaike Government. The UNP assumed a leading part in the denunciation of the pact. Almost as soon as the pact was signed, the UNP working committee demanded its abrogation.[5] The

2. Interview by the author, May 21, 1962. Similarly, see House, *Debates*, Vol. 38, cols. 892-893.

3. *Progress Through Stability: United National Party Manifesto* (Colombo: United National Party, 1958), pp. 22-24.

4. House, *Debates*, Vol. 38, col. 356.

5. *U.N.P. Journal*, Aug. 9, 1957. Subsequent issues of the party newspaper were largely devoted to attacks on the pact.

UNP attack concentrated on features of the pact which drew a distinction between the North and East and the remainder of the island. Senanayake told a rally sponsored by the UNP to protest the pact that "we oppose a regional division of Ceylon on racial grounds for the solution of this [language] or any other problem."[6] A widely distributed UNP booklet, the cover of which depicted a map of the island with a huge black footprint covering the Tamil areas, denounced the pact's virtual prohibition on Sinhalese colonization in Tamil areas, asserting "the future economic development of the country is in the regions now claimed as Federal Party territory." The agreement on language was also denounced with the claim that if the Sinhalese-only legislation "has any meaning, it means that all the 9 provinces, without exception, should be administered in the Sinhalese language."[7]

The new UNP program, although conceding the use of Tamil, condemned special arrangements for the language in the Northern and Eastern Provinces, contending that provision for Tamil "should not be done regionally, but on an all-island scale, without infringing the principle that Sinhalese should be the only Official Language throughout the Island." The program concluded that the Bandaranaike-Chelvanayakam Pact "will not create harmony between the Sinhalese and the Tamil speaking people but will create a permanent rift and lay the foundation for the creation of two or more States based on racial considerations."[8] The UNP assault on the pact was continued during the 1960 election campaigns, and prior to the second election, in July, the UNP stressed allegations that the SLFP had secretly accepted Federal party conditions in exchange for parliamentary support.[9] The UNP's election propaganda frequently contained implied communal appeals, and after the election Tamil leaders accused the party of waging a communalist campaign.[10]

The UNP and the Federal party found their convictions most directly in conflict on the issue of Sinhalese colonization of predominantly Tamil areas. The state-sponsored development and colonization of the dry zone had been pioneered and promoted by D. S. Senanayake as

6. *Ibid.*, Aug. 23, 1957.
7. *First Step* (Colombo: United National Party, n.d.), pp. 8, 11.
8. *Progress Through Stability*, pp. 24-25.
9. E.g., *Times of Ceylon*, July 17, 1960, and July 18, 1960.
10. E.g., House, *Debates*, Vol. 39, cols. 277-278, 440.

minister of agriculture and lands under the Donoughmore Constitution. When the elder Senanayake moved to the premiership at independence, he intrusted the agriculture and lands portfolio and responsibility for the colonization schemes to his son. Both Senanayakes had long displayed a deep interest in the reclaiming of unutilized land and expansion of peasant agriculture. Colonization became embroiled in the communal problem because many of the projects were located in the sparsely populated Eastern Province. A prohibition on the movement of Sinhalese colonists to the Eastern Province was tantamount to abandonment of the agricultural expansion envisioned by the Senanayakes.

From the UNP standpoint, the Federal party demand that Sinhalese colonization cease in the Tamil areas appeared to assert a claim to a part of Ceylon as inviolate territory of one community, from which members of the other community were arbitrarily excluded. This seemed to represent a dangerous and intolerable division of the land and peoples of Ceylon. Dudley Senanayake argued: "It is anti-national to take up the attitude that any area of Ceylon is to be specifically reserved for any particular community or that any particular community should be excluded from any part of Ceylon." He charged that "it is the Federal Party that is taking a communal stand" on colonization.[11] Senanayake has explained his opposition to the Bandaranaike-Chelvanayakam Pact as directed against the provisions on colonization and claimed that he had not objected to the language agreement.[12] Later, although repeating his party's opposition to exclusion of Sinhalese from east-coast colonization schemes, he declared his willingness to accept a compromise solution which would alleviate Tamil fears.[13]

The UNP has frequently claimed that a solution of the language issue and other problems of communal relations can be achieved only by removing these questions from partisan contention. A major restatement of UNP policy in 1963 repeated almost the exact wording of the language policy formulation of 1958, but added: "Among the matters that need urgent attention the [question of] Language Policy ranks foremost. Our Party has repeatedly suggested that this question be removed from the arena of party politics and a solution sought by an All-

11. *U.N.P. Journal*, April 28, 1961.
12. House, *Debates*, Vol. 38, col. 884.
13. *Ibid.*, Vol. 45, col. 1992.

Parties Conference."[14] The party's 1965 election manifesto promised "a Round Table Conference to discuss ways and means of unifying the nation within the framework of Sinhala as the official language of the State."[15]

While the UNP has sought to come to terms with the language aspirations of the Sinhalese majority, after 1960 some indications emerged of sentiment within the party for a broadening of its appeal to encompass the minority groups, as had been done prior to 1956. After the second 1960 election, a party committee headed by J. R. Jayewardene undertook a study of the causes for the UNP defeat. The exhaustive report of the committee stressed measures to refurbish the image of the party and establish a closer identification with the ordinary people, including greater attention to Sinhalese language and cultural aspirations. In addition, however, the report noted that the party had fared badly among the ethnic minorities, and asked: "Are we for ever to ignore the 24 seats available in the Northern and Eastern Provinces? . . . Are we also to ignore the decisive influence of the Tamil and Indian voters in some of the Electorates [in the Sinhalese majority areas]?" The report suggested review of party policy on language and other matters with a view to enhancing the party's appeal among the minorities.[16] In the 1965 election, for the first time since the eruption of the official language issue, a Tamil UNP candidate was elected to Parliament by a constituency with a Tamil majority, defeating Federal party and Tamil Congress opponents. With the single exception of the election of a Communist candidate in 1956, this was the only instance since 1952 in which a Tamil constituency had returned the candidate of any party other than the exclusively Tamil parties.

The SLFP Government's implementation of language policy

When in the July, 1960, election the Sri Lanka Freedom party came to power under the leadership of Sirimavo Bandaranaike, the

14. *What We Believe* (Colombo: United National Party, 1963), pp. 16-18.

15. *United National Party Manifesto, 1965* (Colombo: United National Party, 1965), p. 10.

16. "Report of the Special Committee Appointed by the Working Committee to Inquire and Report within Three Months Generally on the Last General Election Campaign with Particular Reference to Defects if Any in the Said Campaign and Suggestions for Improvements of Similar Campaigns in the Future" (mimeographed; Colombo, [1960?]), p. 38.

position the new Government would take on the language demands of the Tamils was uncertain. Mrs. Bandaranaike was committed to following the policies of her dead husband. Many Tamils felt that S. W. R. D. Bandaranaike had wished to accommodate Tamil claims and that his interpretation of Sinhalese-only had been milder and more flexible than many alternative interpretations. After earlier declaring their willingness to support an SLFP Government, the Federalist leaders in the July election campaign had worked for the SLFP among Tamils living in the South.[17] The SLFP had fought the election pledged to completing the transition to Sinhalese as the only language of government, but promising to carry out its language policy without creating difficulties for the Tamil-speaking people and hinting that S. W. R. D. Bandaranaike's proposals for the use of Tamil might be revived.[18] The new Government made some conciliatory gestures toward the Tamils. The president of the Ceylon Workers' Congress was appointed to Parliament to represent the Indian Tamil estate workers and the Speech from the Throne opening the new session of Parliament was read for the first time in Tamil as well as in Sinhalese and English. However, the Throne Speech proclaimed the Government's intention to proceed with implementation of the Official Language Act "to make Sinhala in reality the official language of this country by 31st December, 1960."[19] In a statement of policy soon after the Throne Speech, the prime minister underscored her determination not to relent on the deadline despite Tamil protests.[20] Federalist disillusionment led to the 1961 *satyagraha*, which was eventually suppressed by arresting the Federal party leaders and imposing an emergency.

After the 1960 elections, Tamil hopes of securing relaxation of the Sinhalese-only policy appeared to be further from realization than ever before. The new Government embarked on a rigorous implementation of the policy. Legislation was enacted for the progressive substitution of Sinhalese for English in court proceedings.[21] The Tamil Language Act remained inoperative, as regulations necessary to give effect to its

17. House, *Debates*, Vol. 46, col. 1917; and Vol. 48, col. 759.
18. *Śrī Laṅkā Nidahas Paksayē Mātivaraṇa Prakāśanaya, 1960* [*Sri Lanka Freedom Party's Election Manifesto, 1960*] (Colombo: Sri Lanka Freedom Party, 1960), p. 11.
19. *Ceylon Today*, IX, 8 (Aug., 1960), 3.
20. *Ibid.*, p. 11.
21. Language of the Courts Act, No. 3 of 1961.

provisions were not promulgated. The 1962 Speech from the Throne promised: "A vigorous policy of implementation of the Official Language Act will be adopted in Public Administration and in the Courts of Law," without mention of the Tamil Language Act.[22] The use of Sinhalese in the bureaucracy was being promoted with increasing energy. Incentive bonuses and the withholding of periodic salary increases and promotions were used to encourage government employees to study Sinhalese. Public servants appointed since 1956 were required to attain proficiency in Sinhalese within three years of their appointment in order to retain their posts.[23] In 1964, action was commenced to retire compulsorily public servants who had not attempted to pass proficiency examinations in Sinhalese, although severances were held up by a court case until after the 1965 election. In addition, the use of Sinhalese was being introduced into the administration of the Tamil areas at an accelerating rate. A number of Sinhalese public servants were transferred to the Jaffna *kachcheri* late in 1963 to complete a change to the use of Sinhalese by the year's end.[24]

The SLFP after 1960 had adopted a strongly majoritarian outlook, contending its parliamentary majority gave the party a popular mandate to carry out its proposals without heed to dissenting views. An SLFP minister, a nephew of S. W. R. D. Bandaranaike, answered protests over Government actions by asserting that "we have been returned with an absolute mandate to govern the country according to the policy laid down in our manifesto."[25] In seeming fulfilment of decades-old Tamil fears, the SLFP had received its popular mandate without contesting a single Tamil constituency. The SLFP Government tended to regard the Tamils, like the English-educated class and the Christians, as intent on preserving privileges obtained during the colonial era, privileges which the SLFP was determined to destroy. Party spokesmen frequently stressed that the Government was restoring the rights and

22. *Ceylon Today*, XI, 7 (July, 1962), 4.
23. For a summary of the language requirements for public service employment under the Official Language Act, see Ceylon, Public Service Commission, *A Guide to a Career in the Public Service* (Colombo: Government Press, n.d.), pp. 5-6.
24. *Times of Ceylon*, Dec. 11, 1963. The impact on the bureaucracy of the shift to Sinhalese as the language of administration is discussed at greater length in Robert N. Kearney, "Ceylon: The Contemporary Bureaucracy," in Ralph Braibanti and associates, *Asian Bureaucratic Systems Emergent from the British Imperial Tradition* (Durham, N.C.: Duke University Press, 1966), pp. 511-518.
25. House, *Debates*, Vol. 39, col. 920.

serving the interests of the majority, defined on the basis of language and religion. Near the conclusion of her premiership, Mrs. Bandaranaike claimed:

We have removed the disabilities placed on the majority of our people by the foreign ruler. The language and the religion of the majority . . . have been developed and their rightful place ensured. While respecting the rights of minorities, the Government, mindful of its obligations to the majority of the people, has restored their lost rights.[26]

In June, 1964, as its parliamentary majority dwindled, the SLFP combined with the Lanka Sama Samaja party in a coalition and three LSSP members entered the Cabinet. A program agreed to by the coalition partners, largely of Sama Samajist inspiration, indicated that long-delayed action would be taken on the 1958 act providing for the use of Tamil. The program's brief statement on the language question announced that the Official Language Act and Tamil Language Act were to be implemented in a way acceptable to both Sinhalese and Tamils.[27] In a policy speech shortly after the formation of the coalition, Mrs. Bandaranaike argued:

Especially at this time when the Government is bent on following a socialist policy, it is our duty to see that Sinhalese and Tamils are treated satisfactorily. . . . It is the duty of every citizen who wishes the country's progress to see that the language question is solved in a way that will benefit the nation and not try to exploit the situation for political purposes.[28]

The following December, before action was taken on the language question, the coalition Government narrowly lost a vote of confidence in Parliament and an election was called for March, 1965. The 1965 election manifesto of the SLFP promised to complete "all remaining steps" in establishing Sinhalese as the official language, but the neglected Tamil Language Act was also "to be implemented in a manner acceptable to both communities with a view to increasing amity and right understanding between majority and minority groups."[29]

26. "Prime Minister's Independence Day Message," *Ceylon Today*, XIV, 2 (Feb., 1965), 6.
27. *Sri Lanka*, June 20, 1964. On the formation of the coalition, see Robert N. Kearney, "The Marxists and Coalition Government in Ceylon," *Asian Survey*, V, 2 (Feb., 1965), 120-124.
28. *Ceylon News*, July 9, 1964.
29. *Election Manifesto of the Sri Lanka Freedom Party, 1965* (Colombo: Sri Lanka Freedom Party, 1965), p. 7.

Marxist adjustments to Sinhalese-only

Of the three Ceylonese Marxist parties, only the small Viplavakari Lanka Sama Samaja party (VLSSP) embraced Sinhalese as the sole official language prior to the 1956 election. As a part of the victorious MEP coalition, VLSSP members served in the MEP Cabinet until the coalition split apart in 1959. At the breakup of the coalition, the VLSSP assumed the name of the defunct coalition and has since called itself the Mahajana Eksath Peramuna. In the election campaign the following year, the MEP continued to champion Sinhalese-only and, like the UNP, concentrated on denunciations of a claimed alliance between the SLFP and the Federal party.[30]

Although the Marxists were among the early advocates of the governmental use of Sinhalese and Tamil, the Lanka Sama Samaja party, the oldest and largest of the Marxist groups, and the Communist party experienced considerable difficulty in adjusting to the rapid growth of Sinhalese-only sentiment. Both parties had supported swabhasha in preference to the continued use of English as an aspect of the class revolt of the vernacular-educated against the English-educated. The LSSP in 1952 included among its demands: "Use of the National Languages with immediate effect in all spheres of administration."[31] But as the language agitation shifted from the demand for swabhasha to the demand for Sinhalese-only, communal rivalry became an increasingly important element in the language controversy. Typical of the Marxist attitude on communal divisions was the statement: "The cleavages that exist among the communities, both social and political, act as obstructions . . . to the emergence in politics of *class issues* in such a form as may be clearly understood by the people."[32] The language issue as transformed by the rising clamor for Sinhalese-only, the Marxists contended, was used by the capitalist parties "to distract the masses from the real

30. E.g., *Anduren Eliyaṭa: Mahajana Eksat Peramunē Mätivaraṇa Prakāsanaya* [*From Darkness to Light: The Mahajana Eksath Peramuna's Election Manifesto*] (Colombo: Mahajana Eksath Peramuna, 1960).
31. *With the Masses into Action* (Colombo: Lanka Sama Samaja Party, 1953), p. 5.
32. Doric de Souza, *Conspiracy Against the People: An Analysis of the Soulbury Commission Report* (Colombo: Bolshevik-Leninist Party, n.d.), p. 16. (Emphasis in original.) The Bolshevik-Leninist party was formed after a schism in the LSSP in about 1945 and was reunited with the LSSP in 1950.

problems and to gain their support by rousing racial antagonisms."[33] A Sama Samajist senator charged that the issue was intended "to divide the Tamil and Sinhalese workers into two camps."[34] A Communist M.P. attempted to shift the focus of an official language debate from the communal to the class dimension, reminding a speaker who referred to the Sinhalese and Tamil nations of "two other nations, those who speak English and those who do not, in this Island of ours."[35]

As Sinhalese-only enthusiasm mounted late in 1955, LSSP members proposed a constitutional amendment to grant Sinhalese and Tamil parity of status as official languages throughout the island. In proposing the motion in direct conflict with the rising tide of Sinhalese-only sentiment, the LSSP leader, N. M. Perera, declared:

It would have been easy for me and the members of my party to have sponsored the very popular idea, Sinhalese only, and we would have been acclaimed as heroes as a good many others have been.

But our party has taken up a consistent attitude [for both Sinhalese and Tamil]. . . . That position we still adhere to. However unpopular that line of action might be, I am convinced myself of the correctness of our attitude. It might mean going into the political wilderness for some time, but still we the members of the Lanka Sama Samaja Party are prepared to face that.[36]

In the 1956 election, the LSSP and Communist party maintained their commitments to parity of status for the two languages, but were allied by a no-contest pact with the Sri Lanka Freedom party which promised immediate legislation making Sinhalese the sole official language. The two Marxist parties largely avoided the language issue during the election contest. The official language question, the dominant issue of the campaign, was not mentioned in the LSSP election manifesto.[37] With the election victory of the MEP coalition and the immediate introduction of official language legislation, however, both Marxist

33. Leslie Goonewardene, *What We Stand For* (Colombo: Lanka Sama Samaja Party, Feb., 1959), p. 8.
34. Ceylon Senate, *Parliamentary Debates (Hansard)*, Vol. 10, col. 496. A prominent Tamil Sama Samajist has argued that the communal problem is a product of the decay of the capitalist system and can be resolved only with the replacement of capitalism by socialism. V. Karalasingham, *The Way Out for the Tamil Speaking People* (Colombo: Young Socialist Publication, Oct., 1963).
35. House, *Debates*, Vol. 20, col. 2042.
36. *Ibid.*, Vol. 23, col. 574.
37. *Manifesto of the LSSP, Parliamentary General Elections, 1956* (Colombo: Lanka Sama Samaja Party, 1956). Also, see I. D. S. Weerawardana, *Ceylon General Election, 1956* (Colombo: M. D. Gunasena & Co., Ltd., 1960), p. 107.

parties resumed their unambiguous opposition to Sinhalese-only. A Communist M.P., the only Marxist candidate ever elected by a Northern Province constituency, soon after the election asserted:

Justice, democracy and national interest require that the demand of the Tamil-speaking peoples for the right to use Tamil as an official language must be recognized. The Communist Party is committed to press and fight for this demand, and as a Communist I must and shall oppose all attempts to deny this right.[38]

The Communists and Sama Samajists joined members of the Federal party and Tamil Congress in voting against the Official Language Act. The rapid escalation of communal tensions and outbreaks of violence following passage of the act brought sharp Marxist condemnations of the MEP Government and denunciations of its "communalist" policies.[39]

Both the LSSP and the Communist party recognized that they suffered political reversals on the language issue. An official LSSP history observed that "the party has paid a heavy price for its stand. It lost heavily among the Sinhalese masses."[40] By 1960, the Communist party had shifted to a policy of Sinhalese as the only "state language," with the Tamil language to be used in education and administration in the Tamil areas.[41] The extent of Communist consciousness of failure on the language issue was revealed at a party congress held after the two elections of 1960. The Communists confessed that they had failed to participate in the language movement because of a "sectarian attitude towards the national and national-cultural struggles." Consequently, "when the struggle over the official language matured in 1956, the Party endorsed wrong slogans and adopted incorrect tactics which temporarily isolated it from the developing movement." In its earlier policy of parity, the Communists admitted, the party had "proceeded from a cosmopolitan and not a Marxist-Leninist understanding."[42]

38. House, *Debates*, Vol. 24, col. 308.
39. A speech in Parliament by a leading Sama Samajist attacking the MEP Government for exacerbating communal tensions was reprinted as a pamphlet by the LSSP: Colvin R. de Silva, *The Failure of Communalist Politics* (Colombo: Lanka Sama Samaja Party, Aug., 1958).
40. Leslie Goonewardene, *A Short History of the Lanka Sama Samaja Party* (Colombo: Lanka Sama Samaja Party, 1960), p. 54.
41. *Manifesto of the Communist Party* (Colombo: Communist Party, 1960), p. 7.
42. *Draft Thesis for the 6th National Congress of the Ceylon Communist Party* (Colombo: Communist Party, 1960), pp. 25-26.

The 1960 elections found the LSSP claiming: "We are justly proud of the fact that we are the only non-communal political party in the country," and calling for Tamil to be made an official language along with Sinhalese.[43] In the July, 1960, election the LSSP again was allied by a no-contest pact to the SLFP and was pledged to support an SLFP Government, although the SLFP was firmly committed to a Sinhalese-only policy. Less than a year later, a party statement on the language issue condemned Government suppression of the Federal party *satyagraha* and demanded action by the Government to "satisfy the just Language claims of the Tamil-speaking people." The statement concluded that "the democratic rights of the people as a whole are imperilled by the failure to bring the language question to a just settlement."[44]

In 1963, the three Marxist parties came together briefly in a United Left Front combining the LSSP, which continued to advocate two official languages, with the Communist party and the Mahajana Eksath Peramuna (the former VLSSP), which had taken Sinhalese-only positions. The common program of the front, after attacking the continued use of English, accepted the Sinhalese-only statute but urged the use of Tamil for some administrative purposes in the North and East as envisaged under the Tamil Language Act.[45] The LSSP had for the first time retreated from its stand for parity of status for the two languages, the last party active in the Sinhalese areas to do so. Less than a year later the United Left Front collapsed and the SLFP-LSSP coalition was formed. The coalition program and the 1965 election manifesto of the SLFP, to which the LSSP also subscribed, repeated acceptance of the existing Sinhalese-only legislation. LSSP members justified the shift by contending that the Tamil leaders themselves had implicitly accepted Sinhalese as the sole official language in agreeing to the Bandaranaike-Chelvanayakam Pact. Thus, the Sama Samajists argued, they had been demanding more for the Tamil language than had the Tamil politicians.[46]

43. *Election Manifesto of the Lanka Sama Samaja Party* (Colombo: Lanka Sama Samaja Party, 1960), pp. 2, 4.

44. "Statement by Parliamentary Group of the Lanka Samasamaja Party (Ceylonese Section of the Fourth International) on the Language Question," *Fourth International*, No. 13 (Spring-Summer, 1961), p. 46.

45. *United Left Front Agreement* (Colombo: Lanka Press, 1963), pp. 9-10.

46. This argument was presented to the author in several conversations with Sama Samajists in 1965.

When the LSSP joined the coalition with the SLFP in 1964, a small group of Sama Samajists broke with the LSSP, contending that collaboration with the "bourgeois" SLFP compromised the party's Trotskyist principles. The dissidents, calling themselves the Lanka Sama Samaja party (Revolutionary), continued to insist on equal status for the Tamil language and stressed the need for just treatment for the minorities.[47]

The National Government and the opposition's "communal line"

A sharp reversal of Tamil political fortunes and brightened prospects for an enduring settlement of the official language issue followed an election on March 22, 1965. The election produced a self-proclaimed "National Government" which included in its ranks both the Federal party and the Tamil Congress. For the first time since 1956, a Tamil served as a minister in the Cabinet. In January, 1966, the first provisions were announced for the use of Tamil since the original enactment of legislation on the official language almost ten years earlier. In its second Speech from the Throne after a year in office, the National Government claimed it had "achieved national unity and maintained the objectives of justice and fair play to all, irrespective of race, community or religion."[48]

The 1965 election followed the defeat of the SLFP-LSSP coalition Government in Parliament on a confidence motion when more than a dozen SLFP M.P.'s deserted the party and crossed to the opposition. From the formation of the coalition in June, 1964, through the election campaign, communal questions were submerged by controversy concerning the coalition's socialist aims, alleged dictatorial actions and designs, and attitude toward Buddhism. The election was bitterly contested. Supporters of the SLFP-LSSP coalition, with which the Communist party was allied,[49] claimed they were combating the final effort of class privilege to maintain itself, and opponents argued that the island faced its last opportunity to preserve democracy and the rule of law. With most

47. E.g., *Election Manifesto of the Lanka Sama Samaja Party (Revolutionary)*, *Parliamentary Elections, 1965* (Colombo: Lanka Sama Samaja Party [Revolutionary], 1965).

48. *Ceylon Today*, XV, 7 (July, 1966), 1.

49. With the election, the Communist party seems to have become an accepted member of the coalition. Communists were included in joint coalition campaign organizations and have participated in coalition activities following the election.

Sinhalese politicians concentrating on other matters, communal issues appeared to play a smaller role in 1965 than in any of the preceding three elections.

The coalition was defeated in the election, the three allied parties capturing a total of 55 of 151 elective seats in the House of Representatives. The UNP, winning 66 seats, was the largest single party but lacked a majority. The National Government was formed around the nucleus of the UNP with Dudley Senanayake as prime minister. In addition, the Government included the Federalists, the Tamil Congress, five M.P.'s who had left the SLFP and grouped together as the Sri Lanka Freedom Socialist party, and the single members of the MEP and the Jathika Vimukthi Peramuna. The last party was once identified as among the most passionate and determined opponents of a language accord with the Tamils. Also supporting the National Government were two officers of the Ceylon Workers' Congress, who were named appointed M.P.'s. A leading Federalist, M. Tiruchelvam, a former solicitor-general of Ceylon, was appointed to the Senate and named minister of local government. This portfolio was of interest to the Tamils because of concern with the language in which local government bodies conduct their affairs and correspond with the central government and possible extension of the functions of local government to meet Tamil desires for autonomy. G. G. Ponnambalam, the Tamil Congress leader, was also offered a Cabinet post but declined it.

Ponnambalam was known to be politically and personally close to the UNP leadership and the Tamil Congress was generally expected to support a Government formed by the UNP. The Federalists, who had been continuously in opposition since the party was formed in 1949, were intent on obtaining a language settlement by use of their parliamentary strength and position and were not committed to either the UNP or the parties forming the coalition. In December, 1964, and again immediately after the election, their support had been solicited by coalition leaders, and they believed that they could have obtained the same settlement from the coalition. Deep bitterness over what they felt to be the SLFP betrayal in 1960 and the insensitivity of the Sirimavo Bandaranaike Government to Tamil interests apparently led them to opt for alliance with the UNP.[50] No formal agreement had been reached

50. E.g., House, *Debates*, Vol. 60, cols. 643-646, 698-701.

with the UNP before the election, but Federal party leaders conceded that the possibility of a coalition with the UNP had been recognized during the campaign. Although previously the Federalists had contemplated merely voting with a Government willing to reach a language settlement, the decision was made to allow a party member to join the Cabinet to give the party a voice in the execution of policy on language and other matters. Furthermore, the presence of a Tamil in the Cabinet was expected to be psychologically satisfying to the Tamil people, who had felt for nearly a decade that they were being ruled by Sinhalese, and to encourage Tamil trust and confidence in the Government.[51]

The National Government moved cautiously on the language question and did not announce its intended measures until early 1966, although it was universally recognized that an accord had been reached between the UNP and the Federal party leaders. The arrangements seemed clearly designed to blunt opposition criticism. The Speech from the Throne announcing the policies of the new Government said only that regulations would be drafted under the two existing language acts, closely paralleling the declaration of the coalition a year earlier.[52] In the ensuing debate, Senanayake repeated the earlier coalition promise that the anticipated regulations would be drafted so as to be acceptable to both communities.[53] The settlement took the form of regulations made under the Tamil Language Act of 1958, which was drafted by S. W. R. D. Bandaranaike.

The regulations, approved by Parliament on January 11, 1966, specified that Tamil is to be used in the Northern and Eastern Provinces "for the transaction of all Government and public business and the maintenance of public records," for communication between Northern and Eastern Province local government bodies and the central government, and throughout the island for correspondence between government officials and private individuals who were educated in Tamil. Furthermore, all statutes, proclamations, notifications, forms, and other publications issued or used by public bodies are to be translated and published in Tamil as well as Sinhalese. Incorporated in the regulations was the assertion that the use of Tamil for the specified purposes was to

51. Interview with Senator M. Tiruchelvam, July 2, 1965.
52. *Ceylon Today*, XIV, 3-4 (March-April, 1965), 10. For the comparable provision of the coalition's Throne Speech, see *ibid.*, XIII, 7 (July, 1964), 1.
53. *Siyarata*, May 21, 1965.

be "without prejudice to the operation of the Official Language Act No. 22 of 1956, which declared the Sinhala language to be the one official language of Ceylon."[54]

In addition to the promulgation of regulations for the first time defining an official use for Tamil, notices of compulsory retirement of public servants on language grounds served before the election were withdrawn. Agreement was also reported on bureaucratic recruitment by which public service examinations were to be conducted in both Sinhalese and Tamil. Public servants appointed on the basis of examinations in Tamil would be required to pass examinations in Sinhalese within three years of appointment, while those appointed through examination in Sinhalese would be required to pass examinations in Tamil in order to serve in the Northern and Eastern Provinces.[55]

The Federalists also expected to obtain some greater degree of local self-government under bodies similar to the regional councils envisaged in the Bandaranaike-Chelvanayakam Pact. The establishment of district councils which would "function under the control and direction of the Central Government," mentioned in the National Government's first Throne Speech, was promised in 1966.[56] The reference to central government control presumably was intended to establish clearly that the councils were not to constitute units of a federal system. During the debate on the Tamil language regulations, Prime Minister Senanayake had announced that legislation creating district councils was soon to be introduced.[57]

Despite a frequent note of intransigence in their public pronouncements, the Federalists by 1965 tended to be realistic in their appraisal of the terms of settlement that could be obtained from a party primarily dependent on Sinhalese votes. As a minimum, the Federalists have insisted that Tamil should be used in the administration of the North and East and that Tamils throughout the island should be able to correspond with the government or compete for public service posts in the Tamil language. They were prepared to concede the principle that Sin-

54. The text of the regulations appears in Appendix IV.
55. Reported in conversations with members of the parties forming the National Government.
56. *Ceylon Today*, XIV, 3-4 (March-April, 1965), 15; *ibid.*, XV, 7 (July, 1966), 8. The coalition government had previously promised to establish district councils, which would cover a smaller area and have less autonomy than the regional councils proposed by Bandaranaike in 1957.
57. *Ceylon Daily News*, Jan. 12, 1966.

halese was the only official language. Senator Tiruchelvam argued soon
after the formation of the National Government that Sinhalese aspirations for their language to be the sole official language and Tamil desires to be governed in their own language in the Tamil areas were not
in conflict. He assured the opposition that "our Government has no intention to undo the Official Language Act at all."[58] A leading UNP
minister claimed that for the first time the Federalists had accepted the
principle of Sinhalese-only and that Sinhalese would be the official language from one end of the island to the other.[59] The settlement was accepted by the Federalists as meeting their most insistent demands and
as preferable to the previously existing situation. However, they clearly
indicated that they considered the settlement only a temporary solution
and were not abandoning their ultimate aims of federalism and parity
of languages.[60]

An assault on the expected language actions of the National Government was launched immediately after the election by the coalition
parties which formed the opposition. Before Government intentions on
the language question were announced, the opposition charged that the
presence of the Federal party on the Government benches implied the
existence of an agreement detrimental to Sinhalese interests. Coalition
speakers and publications commenced a campaign in which Government
concessions to the Tamil language and partiality toward the Tamils and
other minorities were implied and prominent attention was given to
Federalist activities and objectives. As a typical example, under a banner headline reading "Siṅhala Janatāvata Demaḷa Bhāṣāva?" (Tamil
Language for the Sinhalese Community?), the SLFP weekly newspaper implied in reporting a Federalist speech in the North that the
Tamil language might be forced on the Sinhalese.[61] Federal party and
Tamil Congress leaders were accused in a Communist publication of
promoting communalism and using language appeals to the Tamil people to protect reactionary class interests in collusion with the Sinhalese
bourgeoisie.[62] The announcement of the Tamil language regulations

58. Senate, *Debates*, Vol. 22, cols. 628, 631.
59. Speech by J. R. Jayewardene, as reported in *Ceylon Daily News*, July 28, 1965.
60. E.g., *ibid.*, June 7, 1965; House, *Debates*, Vol. 60, col. 683.
61. *Siṅhalē*, Aug. 8, 1965.
62. I. R. Ariyaratnam, "Thirty Years of Communal Politics," *Forward*, July 2,
1965.

early in 1966 produced a joint statement by the leaders of the three coalition parties charging that the regulations "undermine the Official Language Act and will prevent Sinhala from becoming in fact the official language throughout Ceylon." The statement claimed the regulations proved that "the leaders of the UNP have accepted the fundamental aims of the Tamil Arasu Kadchi [Federal party] which seeks to divide Ceylon into two separate and distinct state units."[63] Demonstrations and disorders accompanied a political strike called by coalition supporters to protest the language regulations.[64] The opposition attack emphasizing communal questions and alleging the Government's betrayal of the principle of Sinhalese-only became known as the "communal line."

From post-election evaluations, members of the SLFP-Marxist coalition concluded that coalition candidates had won considerable support among the Sinhalese Buddhists, but that their opponents had received heavy support from ethnic and religious minorities.[65] Loss of the bitterly contested and fairly close election contest was a deep disappointment to many coalitionists, who tended to place the blame for their defeat on the minorities and to identify the National Government with the minorities. The attack on the Government by utilizing language and communal issues appeared to be almost automatic. Denunciations of the minorities reportedly erupted from rank-and-file coalition supporters at the first announcement of the election results and were repeated at a coalition-sponsored May Day rally.

The possibility of exploiting Sinhalese reaction to the presence of the Federal party in the Government and the anticipated announcement of a language settlement must have readily suggested itself to the opposition. The Federal party was the second largest group in the Government, and the Government appeared unlikely to be able to survive without the support of the Tamil M.P.'s. The link between the UNP and the Federal party appeared to be the most vulnerable point at which to attack the Government. The obvious way to drive a wedge between

63. *Ceylon Daily News*, Jan. 5, 1966.
64. *Ibid.*, Jan. 7 and 9, 1966.
65. See the analyses of election returns by LSSP Senator Doric de Souza, *ibid.*, May 27, 1965, and Senate, *Debates*, Vol. 22, cols. 685-697. The LSSP politbureau, in analyzing the election, similarly concluded that the opposition of ethnic and religious minorities was a major cause of the coalition defeat. *Samasamājaya*, July, 1965, p. 4.

the UNP and the Federalists was to create an atmosphere in which the UNP would find it difficult or impossible to accede to Tamil requirements on the language issue. A Tamil senator accused the opposition of attempting to block a language settlement "because they think that the only way in which the Sri Lanka Freedom Party can come back to power is by raising this communal question, by keeping alive the language question, and keeping alive all the political problems of the minorities in this country."[66] A decade of partisan exploitation of communal sentiments associated with the official language demonstrated the political difficulties of attempting an accommodation on the language question. The UNP was warned by an SLFP leader: "There is no Sinhalese Party in this country, be it the United National Party or the Sri Lanka Freedom Party, that can afford [to] concede demands of the type they [the Federalists] are making."[67]

The SLFP probably faced little difficulty in determining the line of attack against the Government. Since its emergence from the Sinhala Maha Sabha, the SLFP had been almost entirely a Sinhalese party and had focused its appeal on the Sinhalese Buddhists. The party has included a few Moors and occasionally contested a Moor constituency, but it has almost totally ignored the Tamils. The SLFP was an early advocate of Sinhalese-only and has sought to preserve its image as the champion of the Sinhalese language and the aspirations of the Sinhalese community. Although S. W. R. D. Bandaranaike was thought to have desired an accord with the Tamils, Sirimavo Bandaranaike's Government appeared to be indifferent to Tamil claims. An attack on the UNP for its presumed concessions to the Federalists and its association with other minority representatives did not involve a risk of alienating supporters or require a sharp reversal of position. Soon after the National Government was formed, an SLFP spokesman warned that "we are not going to allow you to make at the expense of the Sinhalese nation or race any unprincipled agreement as the price of your support [by the Tamil M.P.'s]." He also criticized the inclusion of a Tamil in the Cab-

66. Senate, *Debates*, Vol. 22, cols. 497-498. One coalition supporter who had previously favored granting Tamil language demands told the author that the National Government had been able to come to power because of its agreement on the language question and asked, "Why should we save this Government embarrassment?"
67. House, *Debates*, Vol. 60, col. 903.

inet, expressing concern over the difficulties a Sinhalese-speaking person might experience in attempting to communicate with a Tamil minister.[68]

The "communal line" created much greater difficulties for the LSSP, which for a number of years had been demanding parity of status for the Tamil language and denouncing the communal tactics of other parties. Because of its earlier defense of minority rights, notably at the times of greatest communal tensions in 1955-1956 and 1958, the LSSP had probably received the support of a considerable proportion of the Ceylon and Indian Tamils in the Southwest. With the coalition's adoption of communal arguments, the party lost a number of its Tamil members and supporters, and several LSSP trade unions—particularly the large Lanka Estate Workers' Union which included a sizable Indian Tamil membership—experienced an exodus of Tamil-speaking members.[69] Many Sinhalese Sama Samajists appeared to be embarrassed by or ambivalent toward the "communal line," and considerable confusion seemed to prevail among the party's sympathizers and trade union following. The "communal line" was subjected to vigorous denunciation by the "Revolutionary" section of the LSSP which had split from the party on the formation of the 1964 coalition.[70]

The adoption of the "communal line" followed deep Sama Samajist disappointment in the election defeat of the coalition.[71] The LSSP, the oldest political party in Ceylon, had in its thirty years of existence met repeated frustrations in its quest for power and had been unable to increase its strength appreciably in the seventeen years since independence. The decision to enter the coalition in 1964, following a heated intra-party debate, was reportedly backed by younger members of the party who saw the move as a way out of the impasse in which the party found itself and as a new approach to the party's ultimate objectives. Although much smaller than the SLFP, the LSSP's superior cohesion, discipline, leadership talent, and clarity of purpose created the possibility of great

68. *Ibid.*, Vol. 60, cols. 197, 200.

69. E.g., *Ceylon Daily News*, May 31, 1965; Aug. 2, 1965; Dec. 20, 1965; and Feb. 18, 1966.

70. A detailed attack on the "line," citing numerous statements with a communal flavor in the LSSP and Communist press, by a member of the "Revolutionary" LSSP appears in Sydney Wanasinghe, "From Marxism to Communalism," *Young Socialist* (Colombo), III, 3 (June, 1965), 113-125. Also, see *CMU Bulletin*, May, 1965, p. 2.

71. The following interpretation is a product of numerous conversations with LSSP members and former members during mid-1965.

if not eventually dominant Sama Samajist influence in the coalition. Victory in the 1965 election, Sama Samajists felt, would give the coalition five years within which to work major reforms which would significantly alter the social structure and economic system of the island and break the political strength of the privileged classes. Thereafter, rapid progress toward the party's ultimate social and economic goals would be possible. These prospects were shattered by the election reverse. Some Sama Samajists attributed the margin of defeat to the very minority groups whose interests they had defended at the cost of political setbacks and at times physical violence.

Furthermore, the National Government was dominated by the UNP, which Marxists had long identified with the implacable class enemy. LSSP leaders claimed that once power was firmly in the hands of the UNP, the Government would resort to repression to crush their movement and preclude a future Marxist bid for power. With the Federalists backing the Government and announcement of a language agreement imminent, the "communal line" offered the greatest prospects of success in weakening or toppling the Government. It was presumed that the SLFP would employ Sinhalese communal and language sentiments against the Government. In order to preserve coalition unity, which was important to the future plans of at least a major segment of the LSSP leadership, a common strategy of opposition seemed necessary. The result was that the language agreement and the communal composition and backing of the Government became the opposition's principal avenues of attack.

With the opposition emphasis on communal themes in the hope of splitting the Sinhalese and Tamil supporters of the Government or creating a strong Sinhalese reaction against the UNP, the problems of communal relations and the official language again became central issues of Ceylonese politics. While the success of the opposition strategy and the durability of the language settlement remain to be determined, the developments following the 1965 election demonstrated the continuing role played in Ceylonese politics by communal sentiments and the official language issue.

Conclusion

The peoples of Ceylon have been divided into separate and exclusive communities differentiated by language, religion, culture, and myth of origin for at least a thousand years. The considerable social and economic changes of the last 150 years created integrative institutions in which Sinhalese and Tamils interacted and developed common interests and outlooks, produced new occupations and classes which cut across communal lines, and diffused values and ideologies to which communal sentiments were repugnant or irrelevant. Communal identification and solidarity remained, however, as an important social reality. Modernizing influences and changing values and practices had not dislodged the community as the largest social group with which the individual could establish a close sense of identification. Except among the most cosmopolitan of the urban middle class, an image of the Ceylonese people embracing both Sinhalese and Tamils remained at best blurred and ill-defined and one with which few of either major community could establish a satisfying identification. It was much easier for the Sinhalese to seek their identity in the Sinhalese language, in Buddhism, and in the traditions of the *Mahāvamsa*, an identity sharpened and popularized by the Buddhist revival and the resurgence of Sinhalese self-awareness at the end of the nineteenth century.

Modern communalism in Ceylon has been pre-eminently a political phenomenon. Political change accompanying the other facets of modernization involved the creation of a modern active state, independence from foreign rule, mass participation in politics, and competition for power through political parties and elections. The lingering popular sense of communal identification and solidarity became of increasing political significance as the franchise was extended and power began to shift from colonial administrators to elected Ceylonese representatives. The approach of self-government produced the first major indications of communal rivalry in modern times as concern developed for the relative political strength of the communities after the removal of foreign control, a concern based on the assumption that power possessed by members of one community would be used for the exclusive benefit of that community. In an era in which the state has become almost universally recognized as the final arbiter of conflicting interests and the chief device for realizing collective goals, it is scarcely surprising that communal interests and aspirations should be pursued in the political arena.

After independence, the official language question became the central issue of communal rivalry, producing a serious rupture of communal relations and posing a threat to the unity of Ceylon. The language controversy was related to the modernizing social, political, and ideological changes occurring on the island. The demand for an exclusive status for the Sinhalese language was a consequence of the growth of a political process based on mass participation. The swabhasha movement arose from a popular desire to end the exclusive privilege of the small English-educated class and instal the people's own language as the official language and the language of social and economic opportunity. Demands that channels of access to new opportunities and modern urban careers be opened to wider segments of the population reflected changing values and aspirations. Recognition of a superior status for the language of the people was intended to facilitate the incorporation of the masses into the effective life of the polity. The official language issue turned into a communally divisive controversy because there was not one single language or identity which included all the Ceylonese people. The search for a wider identity had stopped at the boundaries of the community. Hence, it was a simple transition from the demand for swabhasha to the exclusive demand for Sinhalese, the language of the majority of the people and all who were included within the emotional bonds of the community. Although the recent growth of communal competition is linked to social and political developments accompanying the process of modernization, communalism constitutes a major obstacle to the continued process of modernization by retarding the emergence of a concept of nationality or citizenship based not on ascriptive primordial group membership but on voluntary association and participation in a civil polity.

While it did not arise primarily as a communal dispute, the official language issue possessed profound communal implications and great potential for mobilizing communal support. Language is one of the most

important factors separating the two major communities and is fundamental to the self-identification of each. As communal solidarity was
aroused, the communal distribution of opportunities for government employment and social advancement became intertwined with the psychological satisfactions to be derived from recognition of a special status
for one's own language and a pre-eminent position for one's own people.
For both communities, the language issue came to symbolize the basic
competition between communities. To the Sinhalese, the issue involved
their aspirations to retrieve their cultural heritage and reassert their
position as the majority of the island's people. To the Tamils, the language dispute demonstrated the inherent dangers of Sinhalese domination and the helplessness of their community before the Sinhalese
majority.

The abandonment of communal electorates before independence was
predicated on the expectation that legislators elected territorially and
political parties competing for power would seek to accommodate diverse
communal as well as other interests. Thus, it was argued, mass suffrage
and a competitive political process could contribute to the integration
of the peoples of Ceylon. However, the rise and triumph of the demand
for Sinhalese-only demonstrated that where the deeply felt aspirations
of the two communities collided, the Sinhalese numerical preponderance
was great enough that the desires of the Tamils could be ignored. For
nearly ten years almost no concession was made to impassioned Tamil
opinion by Cabinets composed entirely of Sinhalese. Political parties had
never had great success in attracting support from both communities.
The intensity of Sinhalese-only sentiment required parties competing for
Sinhalese votes to adopt a language policy which effectively excluded
them from bidding for Tamil support. The Tamil community reacted to
the language controversy by retreating more completely into support of
exclusively Tamil parties. After 1956, only the Marxists attempted to
compete for support among both Sinhalese and Tamils. The Marxists,
motivated by an ideology which denies the relevance of communal identifications, resisted for a time the intrusion of the language controversy,
but the imperatives of Sinhalese numerical predominance and official
language aspirations led them as well to eventual adoption of a Sinhalese-only policy. The success of the language issue in mobilizing Sinhalese support led to partisan competition in espousing most vigorously the

demands of the Sinhalese majority. Electoral competition tended to force political parties other than exclusively Tamil parties into increasingly rigorous adherence to Sinhalese-only. Accommodation of Tamil interests was prevented for nearly a decade by each party's need to appear as an uncompromising champion of Sinhalese aspirations. Compulsions of competitive politics and the need to form a parliamentary majority did, however, contribute to agreement in 1965 on the first official provision for the use of the Tamil language and installation of the first Tamil to serve in the Cabinet since the commencement of the official language controversy. The speed and vigor with which the opposition seized on the language accord as a means of attacking the Government indicated the continuing importance of language appeals and communal sentiments in political competition.

Growing rivalry between communities has been accompanied by some tendency toward a reduction of divisions within the communities. Particularly in the Tamil community, which as the minority has been more engrossed in the question of communal relations, the contest between communities has produced efforts to reduce caste distinctions and regional differences in the interest of Tamil unity and solidarity. Although less prominent, parallel tendencies seem to have been present in the Sinhalese community. The first major Sinhalese communal organization, the Sinhala Maha Sabha, professed to seek the unity of the Sinhalese above caste or regional divisions. The emergence of the larger community as the principal focus of loyalty and solidarity may tend to eclipse the smaller sub-communal identifications based on caste, kin, and locality.

Despite the spiraling of communal tensions and emotions inflamed by the language issue, the political gulf between communities has not approached a total break. Bargaining between Sinhalese and Tamil political leaders has occurred almost continuously. To a considerable extent, the communal struggle has been fought out within the common institution of Parliament, where spokesmen of both communities argue their causes within the same chambers, according to the same rules of procedure, and, although with declining frequency, often in the common language of English. Since 1958 communal rivalry has not deteriorated into mob violence. There is slight indication among the Tamils of sentiment for total political separation either as an independent state or as a part of a wider Tamil or Dravidian state. Few Sinhalese seem prepared to deny to the Ceylon Tamils membership in the Ceylonese polity, although the Indian Tamils were readily excluded. After nearly a decade of language strife, a predominantly Sinhalese Government accepted the need for a language accommodation satisfactory to the Tamils and political co-operation with the Tamil leaders. Although other issues and other lines of division frequently emerge, the enduring strength of identification with the community and the potential of communal sentiments for mobilizing political support nonetheless remain of manifest and undisputed significance in the contemporary politics of Ceylon.

The Official Language Act, No. 33 of 1956*

An Act to prescribe the Sinhala Language as the One Official Language of Ceylon and to enable certain transitory provisions to be made.

(Date of Assent: July 7, 1956)

Be it enacted by the Queen's Most Excellent Majesty by and with the advice and consent of the Senate and the House of Representatives of Ceylon in this present Parliament assembled, and by the authority of the same, as follows:—

Short Title

1. This Act may be cited as the Official Language Act, No. 33 of 1956.

Sinhala language to be the one official language

2. The Sinhala language shall be the one official language of Ceylon:

Provided that where the Minister considers it impracticable to commence the use of only the Sinhala language for any official purpose immediately on the coming into force of this Act, the language or languages hitherto used for that purpose may be continued to be so used until the necessary change is effected as early as possible before the expiry of the thirty-first of December, 1960, and, if such change cannot be effected by administrative order, regulations may be made under this Act to effect such change.

Regulations

3. (1) The Minister may make regulations in respect of all matters for which regulations are authorized by this Act to be made and generally for the purpose of giving effect to the principles and provisions of this Act.

(2) No regulation made under sub-section (1) shall have effect until it is approved by the Senate and the House of Representatives and notification of such approval is published in the *Gazette*.

*Text from Ceylon, Department of Information, *The Official Language and the Reasonable Use of Tamil* (Colombo: Government Press, n.d.), pp. 39-40.

The "Bandaranaike-Chelvanayakam Pact," July 26, 1957*

Text of Joint Statements by Prime Minister and Representatives of the Federal Party

The following are the two joint statements issued by the Prime Minister and Representatives of the Federal Party on July 26:

Statement on the general principles of the Agreement between the Prime Minister and the Federal Party

"Representatives of the Federal Party have had a series of discussions with the Prime Minister in an effort to resolve the differences of opinion that had been growing and creating tension.

"At an early stage of these conversations it became evident that it was not possible for the Prime Minister to accede to some of the demands of the Federal Party.

"The Prime Minister stated that from the point of view of the Government he was not in a position to discuss the setting up of a federal constitution or regional autonomy or any step which would abrogate the Official Language Act. The question then arose whether it was possible to explore the possibility of an adjustment without the Federal Party abandoning or surrendering any of its fundamental principles and objectives.

"At this stage the Prime Minister suggested an examination of the Government's draft Regional Councils Bill to see whether provision could be made under it to meet reasonably some of the matters in this regard which the Federal Party had in view.

"The agreements so reached are embodied in a separate document.

"Regarding the language issue the Federal Party reiterated its stand for parity, but in view of the position of the Prime Minister in this matter they came to an agreement by way of an adjustment. They pointed out that it was important for them that there should be a recognition of Tamil as a national language and that the administrative work in the Northern and Eastern Provinces should be done in Tamil.

*The text is taken from Ceylon, House of Representatives, *Parliamentary Debates (Hansard)*, Vol. 30, cols. 1309-1311.

"The Prime Minister stated that as mentioned by him earlier it was not possible for him to take any step which would abrogate the Official Language Act.

Use of Tamil] "After discussions it was agreed that the proposed legislation should contain recognition of Tamil as the language of a national minority of Ceylon, and that the four points mentioned by the Prime Minister should include provision that, without infringing on the position of the Official Language Act, the language of administration in the Northern and Eastern Provinces should be Tamil and that any necessary provision be made for the non-Tamil speaking minorities in the Northern and Eastern Provinces.

"Regarding the question of Ceylon citizenship for people of Indian descent and revision of the Citizenship Act, the representatives of the Federal Party put forward their views to the Prime Minister and pressed for an early settlement.

"The Prime Minister indicated that this problem would receive early consideration.

"In view of these conclusions the Federal Party stated that they were withdrawing their proposed satyagraha."

Joint Statement by the Prime Minister and Representatives of the Federal Party on Regional Councils

"(A) Regional areas to be defined in the Bill itself by embodying them in a schedule thereto.

"(B) That the Northern Province is to form one Regional area whilst the Eastern Province is to be divided into two or more Regional areas.

"(C) Provision is to be made in the Bill to enable two or more regions to amalgamate even beyond provincial limits; and for one region to divide itself subject to ratification by Parliament. Further provision is to be made in the Bill for two or more regions to collaborate for specific purposes of common interest.

Direct Elections] "(D) Provision is to be made for direct election of regional councillors. Provision is to be made for a delimitation Commission or Commissions for carving out electorates. The question of M.P.'s representing districts falling within regional areas to be eligible to function as chairmen is to be considered. The question of Government Agents being Regional Commissioners is to be considered. The question of supervisory functions over larger towns, strategic towns and municipalities is to be looked into.

Special Powers] "(E) Parliament is to delegate powers and to specify them in the Act. It was agreed that Regional Councils should have powers over specified subjects including agriculture, co-operatives, lands and land development, colonization, education, health, industries and fisheries, housing and social services, electricity, water schemes and roads. Requisite definition of powers will be made in the Bill.

Colonisation Schemes] "(F) It was agreed that in the matter of colonisation schemes the powers of the Regional Councils shall include the power to select allottees to whom lands within their area of authority shall be alienated and also power to select personnel to be employed for work on such schemes. The position regarding the area at present administered by the Gal Oya Board in this matter requires consideration.

Taxation, Borrowing] "(G) The powers in regard to the Regional Councils vested in the Minister of Local Government in the draft Bill to be revised with a view to vesting control in Parliament wherever necessary.

"(H) The Central Government will provide block grants to the Regional Councils. The principles on which the grants will be computed will be gone into. The Regional Councils shall have powers of taxation and borrowing."

The Tamil Language (Special Provisions) Act, No. 28 of 1958*

An Act to make provision for the use of the Tamil language and to provide for matters connected therewith or incidental thereto.

(Date of Assent: September 4, 1958)

Whereas the Sinhala language has been declared by the Official Language Act, No. 33 of 1956, to be the one official language of Ceylon:

And whereas it is expedient to make provision for the use of the Tamil language without conflicting with the provisions of the aforesaid Act:

Be it enacted by the Queen's Most Excellent Majesty, by and with the advice and consent of the Senate and the House of Representatives of Ceylon in this present Parliament assembled, and by the authority of the same, as follows:—

Short Title

1. This Act may be cited as the Tamil Language (Special Provisions) Act, No. 28 of 1958.

Tamil language as a medium of instruction

2. (1) A Tamil pupil in a Government school or an Assisted school shall be entitled to be instructed through the medium of the Tamil language in accordance with such regulations under the Education Ordinance, No. 31 of 1939, relating to the medium of instruction as are in force or may hereafter be brought into force.

(2) When the Sinhala language is made a medium of instruction in the University of Ceylon, the Tamil language shall, in accordance with the provisions of the Ceylon University Ordinance, No. 20 of 1942, and of the Statutes, Acts and Regulations made thereunder, be made a medium of instruction in such University for students who, prior to their admission to such University, have been educated through the medium of the Tamil language.

*Text from Ceylon, Department of Information, *The Official Language and the Reasonable Use of Tamil* (Colombo: Government Press, n.d.), pp. 41-44.

Tamil language as a medium of examination for admission to the Public Service

3. A person educated through the medium of the Tamil language shall be entitled to be examined through such medium at any examination for the admission of persons to the Public Service, subject to the condition that he shall, according as regulations made under this Act in that behalf may require,—

    (a) have a sufficient knowledge of the official language of Ceylon, or

    (b) acquire such knowledge within a specified time after admission to the Public Service:

Provided that, when the Government is satisfied that there are sufficient facilities for the teaching of the Sinhala language in schools in which the Tamil language is a medium of instruction and that the annulment of clause (b) of the preceding provisions of this section will not cause undue hardship, provision may be made by regulation made under this Act that such clause shall cease to be in force.

Use of the Tamil language for correspondence

4. Correspondence between persons, other than officials in their official capacity, educated through the medium of the Tamil language and any official in his official capacity or between any local authority in the Northern or Eastern Province and any official in his official capacity may, as prescribed, be in the Tamil language.

Use of the Tamil language for prescribed administrative purposes in the Northern and Eastern Provinces

5. In the Northern and Eastern Provinces the Tamil language may be used for prescribed administrative purposes, in addition to the purposes for which that language may be used in accordance with the other provisions of this Act, without prejudice to the use of the official language of Ceylon in respect of those prescribed administrative purposes.

Regulations

6. (1) The Minister may make regulations to give effect to the principles and provisions of this Act.

    (2) No regulation made under sub-section (1) shall have effect until it is approved by the Senate and the House of Representatives and notification of such approval is published in the *Gazette*.

This Act to be subject to measures adopted or to be adopted under the proviso to section 2 of Act No. 33 of 1956

7. This Act shall have effect subject to such measures as may have been or may be adopted under the proviso to section 2 of the Official Language Act, No. 33, of 1956, during the period ending on the thirty-first day of December, 1960.

Interpretation

8. In this Act unless the context otherwise requires—

"Assisted school" and "Government school" shall have the same meaning as in the Education Ordinance, No. 31 of 1939;

"local authority" means any Municipal Council, Urban Council, Town Council or Village Committee;

"official" means the Governor-General, or any Minister, Parliamentary Secretary or officer of the Public Service; and

"prescribed" means prescribed by regulation made under this Act.

APPENDIX IV

Tamil Language (Special Provisions) Regulations, 1966*

1. These regulations may be cited as the Tamil Language (Special Provisions) Regulations, 1966.

2. Without prejudice to the operation of the Official Language Act No. 33 of 1956, which declared the Sinhala language to be the one official language of Ceylon, the Tamil language shall also be used—

   (a) In the Northern and Eastern Provinces for the transaction of all Government and public business and the maintenance of public records whether such business is conducted in or by a department or institution of the Government[,] a public corporation or a statutory institution; and

   (b) for all correspondence between persons other than officials in their official capacity, educated through the medium of the Tamil language and any official in his official capacity, or between any local authority in the Northern and Eastern Provinces which conducts its business in the Tamil language and any official in his official capacity.

3. For the purpose of giving full force and effect to the principles and provisions of the Tamil Language (Special Provisions) Act, No. 28 of 1958, and these regulations all Ordinances and Acts, and all Orders, Proclamation[s], rules, by-laws, regulations and notifications made or issued under any written law, the Government Gazette and all other official publications, circulars and forms issued or used by the Government, public corporations or statutory institutions, shall be translated and published in the Tamil language also.

*Text from the Department of Information publication *Sri Lanka*, Feb. 1, 1966, p. 4.

BIBLIOGRAPHY

Government Publications

Ceylon. *Administration Report of the Director of Education* for 1935-1945. Colombo: Government Press, 1936-1946.

――――. *Administration Reports of the Government Agents for 1958.* Colombo: Government Press, 1960.

――――. Department of Census and Statistics. *Census of Ceylon, 1946.* Vol. IV. Colombo: Government Press, 1952.

――――. ――――. *Census of Ceylon, 1953.* Vols. I-III. Colombo: Government Press, 1957-1960.

――――. ――――. *Ceylon Year Book,* 1948-1963. Colombo: Government Press, 1949-1964.

――――. ――――. *Statistical Abstract of Ceylon,* 1954-1964. Colombo: Government Press, 1954-1965.

――――. Department of Commerce and Industries. *Annual General Report* for 1920-1937. Colombo: Government Printer, 1921-1938.

――――. ――――. *Report on the Blue Book* for 1917-1919. Colombo: Government Printer, 1918-1920.

――――. Department of Information. *Ceylon Today* (monthly).

――――. ――――. *The Official Language and the Reasonable Use of Tamil.* Colombo: Government Press, n.d.

――――. ――――. *Sri Lanka* (fortnightly).

――――. *Final Report of the National Education Commission, 1961.* Sessional Paper XVII, 1962.

――――. *Final Report of the Official Languages Commission.* Sessional Paper XXII, 1953.

――――. *First Interim Report of the Official Languages Commission.* Sessional Paper XXI, 1951.

――――. House of Representatives. *Parliamentary Debates (Hansard).* Vols. 1-60.

――――. *Interim Report of the Commission of Inquiry into the Outbreaks of Civil Disturbance in the Eastern Province.* Sessional Paper III, 1957.

――――. *Interim Report of the Commission on Higher Education in National Languages.* Sessional Paper XXI, 1954.

――――. Public Service Commission. *A Guide to a Career in the Public Service.* Colombo: Government Press, n.d.

――――. *Report of the Delimitation Commission.* Sessional Paper XV, 1959.

――――. *Report of the Director of Education* for 1912-1930. Colombo: Government Printer, 1913-1931.

————. *Report of the Director of Public Instruction* for 1880-1911. Colombo: Government Printer, 1881-1912.

————. *Report of the First Delimitation Commission Appointed in Accordance with Sub-section (1) of Section 76 of the Ceylon (Constitution) Order in Council, 1946.* Sessional Paper XIII, 1946.

————. *Report of the Kandyan Peasantry Commission.* Sessional Paper XVIII, 1951.

————. *Report to His Excellency the Governor-General by the Commission Appointed in Terms of the Commissions of Inquiry Act to Inquire into and Report on Certain Matters Connected with the Assassination of the Late Prime Minister Solomon West Ridgeway Dias Bandaranaike.* Sessional Paper III, 1965.

————. Senate. *Parliamentary Debates (Hansard).* Vols. 1-22.

————. *Sinhalese and Tamil as Official Languages.* Sessional Paper XXII, 1946.

————. State Council. *Debates in the State Council of Ceylon (Hansard).* 1931-1947.

Great Britain. Colonial Office. *Ceylon: Report of the Commission on Constitutional Reform.* Cmd. 6677. London: His Majesty's Stationery Office, 1945.

——. ——. *Ceylon: Report of the Special Commission on the Constitution.* Cmd. 3131. London: His Majesty's Stationery Office, 1928.

——. ——. *Correspondence Regarding the Constitution of Ceylon.* Cmd. 3419. London: His Majesty's Stationery Office, 1929.

——. ——. *Correspondence Relating to the Constitution of Ceylon.* Cmd. 5910. London: His Majesty's Stationery Office, 1938.

——. ——. *Correspondence Relating to the Further Revision of the Constitution of Ceylon.* Cmd. 1809. London: His Majesty's Stationery Office, 1923.

——. ——. *Further Correspondence Relating to the Revision of the Constitution of Ceylon.* Cmd. 2062. London: His Majesty's Stationery Office, 1924.

Books, Monographs, and Pamphlets

Abhayavardhana, Hector, *et al. The Role of the Western-Educated Elite.* Community Pamphlet No. 1. Colombo: Community Institute, 1962.

Aňduren Eliyaṭa: Mahajana Eksat Peramunē Mātivaraṇa Prakāśanaya [*From Darkness to Light: The Mahajana Eksath Peramuna's Election Manifesto*]. Colombo: Mahajana Eksath Peramuna, 1960.

Arasaratnam, S. *Ceylon.* Englewood Cliffs, N. J.: Prentice-Hall, Inc., 1964.

Bandaranaike, Sirimavo Dias. *Siṅhalayāgē Anāgataya hā Indu Laṅkā Praśnaya* [*The Future of the Sinhalese and the Indo-Ceylon Question*]. Colombo: Jātika Adhyāpana Maṇḍalaya, 1965.

Bandaranaike, S. W. R. D. (ed.). *The Handbook of the Ceylon National Congress, 1919-1928.* Colombo: H. W. Cave & Co., 1928.
———. *Speeches and Writings.* Colombo: Department of Broadcasting and Information, 1963.
———. *Towards a New Era.* Colombo: Department of Information, 1961.
Buddhist Committee of Inquiry. *The Betrayal of Buddhism.* Balangoda, Ceylon: Dharmavijaya Press, 1956.
Cartman, James. *Hinduism in Ceylon.* Colombo: M. D. Gunasena & Co., Ltd., 1957.
The Case for a Federal Constitution for Ceylon: Resolutions Passed at the First National Convention of the Ilankai Tamil Arasu Kadchi. Colombo: Ilankai Tamil Arasu Kadchi, 1951.
Ceylon Daily News. *Parliament of Ceylon, 1947.* Colombo: Associated Newspapers of Ceylon, Ltd., n.d.
———. *Parliament of Ceylon, 1956.* Colombo: Associated Newspapers of Ceylon, Ltd., n.d.
———. *Parliaments of Ceylon, 1960.* Colombo: Associated Newspapers of Ceylon, Ltd., [1962].
Ceylon Faces Crisis. Colombo: Federal Party, 1957.
Ceylon Workers' Congress Report, 1964-1965. Colombo: Ceylon Workers' Congress, n.d.
Chelvanayakam, S. J. V. *Presidential Address Delivered at the Inaugural and First Business Meeting of the Ilankai Tamil Arasu Kadchi on 18th December, 1949.* Colombo: Ilankai Tamil Arasu Kadchi, n.d.
———. *Presidential Address, Ilankai Tamil Arasu Kadchi Ninth National Convention, 1964.* Colombo: Ilankai Tamil Arasu Kadchi, 1964.
Cook, Elsie K. *Ceylon: Its Geography, Its Resources and Its People.* Revised by K. Kularatnam. 2nd ed. Madras: Macmillan and Company, Limited, 1951.
Coomaraswamy, Ananda K. *Medieval Sinhalese Art.* Broad Campden, England: Essex House Press, 1908.
Davy, John. *An Account of the Interior of Ceylon.* London: Longman, Hurst, Rees, Orme, and Brown, 1821.
Denham, E. B. *Ceylon at the Census of 1911.* Colombo: Government Printer, 1912.
De Silva, Colvin R. *The Failure of Communalist Politics.* Colombo: Lanka Sama Samaja Party, August, 1958.
De Silva, K. M. *Social Policy and Missionary Organizations in Ceylon, 1840-1855.* London: Longmans, Green and Co., Ltd., for the Royal Commonwealth Society, 1965.
De Souza, Doric. *Conspiracy Against the People: An Analysis of the Soulbury Commission Report.* Colombo: Bolshevik-Leninist Party, n.d.
Deutsch, Karl W. *Nationalism and Social Communication.* Cambridge, Mass.: M.I.T. Press, 1953.

Dharmapala, Anagarika. *Return to Righteousness*. Edited by Ananda Guruge. Colombo: Anagarika Dharmapala Birth Centenary Committee, Ministry of Education and Cultural Affairs, 1965.

Draft Thesis for the 6th National Congress of the Ceylon Communist Party. Colombo: Communist Party, 1960.

Election Manifesto of the Lanka Sama Samaja Party. Colombo: Lanka Sama Samaja Party, 1960.

Election Manifesto of the Lanka Sama Samaja Party (Revolutionary), Parliamentary Elections, 1965. Colombo: Lanka Sama Samaja Party (Revolutionary), 1965.

Election Manifesto of the Sri Lanka Freedom Party, 1965. Colombo: Sri Lanka Freedom Party, 1965.

Emerson, Rupert. *From Empire to Nation: The Rise to Self-Assertion of Asian and African Peoples*. Boston: Beacon Press, 1960.

Farmer, B. H. *Pioneer Peasant Colonization in Ceylon*. London: Oxford University Press, 1957.

Ferguson, John. *Ceylon in 1903*. Colombo: A. M. & J. Ferguson, 1903.

Fernando, J. L. *Three Prime Ministers of Ceylon: An 'Inside Story.'* Colombo: M. D. Gunasena & Co., Ltd., 1963.

First Step. Colombo: United National Party, n.d.

Goonewardene, Leslie. *A Short History of the Lanka Sama Samaja Party*. Colombo: Lanka Sama Samaja Party, 1960.

————. *What We Stand For*. Colombo: Lanka Sama Samaja Party, February, 1959.

Hulugalle, H. A. J. *The Life and Times of D. R. Wijewardene*. Colombo: Associated Newspapers of Ceylon, Ltd., 1960.

Jayasundera, U. A. (ed.). *United National Party Independence Souvenir, 1951*. Colombo: United National Party, 1951.

Jennings, Sir W. Ivor. *The Constitution of Ceylon*. 3rd ed. London: Oxford University Press, 1953.

————. *The Economy of Ceylon*. 2nd ed. London: Oxford University Press, 1951.

————. *Nationalism and Political Development in Ceylon*. Secretariat Paper No. 10. New York: Institute of Pacific Relations, 1950.

Joint Programme of the Mahajana Eksath Peramuna. Colombo: Mahajana Eksath Peramuna, 1956.

Josey, Alex. *Socialism in Asia*. Singapore: Donald Moore, 1957.

Karalasingham, V. *The Way Out for the Tamil Speaking People*. Colombo: Young Socialist Publication, 1963.

Livingstone, George. *The Tamilians in Ceylon and a Federal Constitution*. Colombo: Ilankai Tamil Arasu Kadchi, n.d.

Ludowyk, E. F. C. *The Footprint of the Buddha*. London: George Allen & Unwin, 1958.

————. *The Story of Ceylon*. London: Faber & Faber, Ltd., 1962.

The Mahāvaṃsa or the Great Chronicle of Ceylon. Translated by Wilhelm Geiger. London: Oxford University Press, 1912.

Manifesto of the Communist Party. Colombo: Communist Party, 1960.

Manifesto of the Ilankai Tamil Arasu Kadchi. Colombo: Ilankai Tamil Arasu Kadchi, 1960.

Manifesto of the LSSP, Parliamentary General Elections, 1956. Colombo: Lanka Sama Samaja Party, 1956.

Mendis, G. C. *Ceylon Today and Yesterday.* 2nd ed. rev. Colombo: Associated Newspapers of Ceylon, Ltd., 1963.

———. *Ceylon Under the British.* 2nd ed. rev. Colombo: Colombo Apothecaries Co., Ltd., 1948.

——— (ed.). *The Colebrooke-Cameron Papers: Documents on British Colonial Policy in Ceylon, 1796-1833.* 2 vols. London: Oxford University Press, 1956.

Mills, Lennox A. *Ceylon Under British Rule, 1795-1932.* London: Oxford University Press, 1933.

Muelder, Wallace R. *Schools for a New Nation.* Colombo: K. V. G. de Silva & Sons, 1962.

Namasivayam, S. *The Legislatures of Ceylon, 1928-1948.* London: Faber & Faber, Ltd., 1951.

———. *Parliamentary Government in Ceylon, 1948-1958.* Colombo: K. V. G. de Silva & Sons, n.d.

Nayar, Baldev Raj. *Minority Politics in the Punjab.* Princeton: Princeton University Press, 1966.

Perera, S. G., S.J. *A History of Ceylon.* Vol. II: *The British Period and After, 1796-1956.* Revised by V. Perniola, S.J. 7th ed. Colombo: Associated Newspapers of Ceylon, Ltd., 1959.

Pillay, K. K. *South India and Ceylon.* Madras: University of Madras, 1963.

Presidential Address of Mr. A. Aziz at the Annual Sessions of the Democratic Workers' Congress Held at Yatiyantota on the 17th of August, 1963. Colombo: Democratic Workers' Congress, n.d.

Progress Through Stability: United National Party Manifesto. Colombo: United National Party, 1958.

Raghavan, M. D. *India in Ceylonese History, Society and Culture.* Bombay: Asia Publishing House, 1964.

———. *The Karāva of Ceylon.* Colombo: K. V. G. de Silva & Sons, 1961.

Rahula, Walpola. *History of Buddhism in Ceylon: The Anuradhapura Period.* Colombo: M. D. Gunasena & Co., Ltd., 1956.

Ramanathan, P. [Sir Ponnambalam]. *Riots and Martial Law in Ceylon, 1915.* London: St. Martin's Press, 1916.

Rasamanickam, S. M. *The Presidential Address at the National Convention of the Ilankai Tamil Arasu Kadchi, 1962.* Colombo: Ilankai Tamil Arasu Kadchi, 1962.

————. *Presidential Address, Ilankai Tamil Arasu Kadchi 7th Annual Convention, 1961.* Jaffna: Ilankai Tamil Arasu Kadchi, 1961.

Ryan, Bryce. *Caste in Modern Ceylon.* New Brunswick, N.J.: Rutgers University Press, 1953.

Sangharakshita, Bhikshu. *Anagarika Dharmapala: A Biographical Sketch.* Kandy: Buddhist Publication Society, 1964.

Saparamadu, S. D. (ed.). *The D. S. Senanayake Memorial Number.* Special issue of *Ceylon Historical Journal,* V, 1-4 (July, 1955-April, 1956).

Sarathchandra, E. R. *The Sinhalese Novel.* Colombo: M. D. Gunasena & Co., Ltd., 1950.

Sarkar, N. K., and S. J. Tambiah. *The Disintegrating Village.* Colombo: Ceylon University Press Board, 1957.

Shils, Edward. *Political Development in the New States.* 's Gravenhage: Mouton & Co., 1962.

Smith, Wilfred Cantwell. *Modern Islam in India.* Lahore: Sh. Muhammad Ashraf, 1963.

Śrī Laṅkā Nidahas Pakṣayē Mātivaraṇa Prakāśanaya, 1960 [Sri Lanka Freedom Party's Election Manifesto, 1960]. Colombo: Sri Lanka Freedom Party, 1960.

United Left Front Agreement. Colombo: Lanka Press, 1963.

United National Party Constitution. Revised September 11, 1948. Colombo: United National Party, 1948.

United National Party Eighth Annual Conference and Mass Rally. Colombo: United National Party, [1956].

United National Party Manifesto, 1965. Colombo: United National Party, 1965.

Vanniasingam, C. *Presidential Address, 1956 Annual Convention of the Ilankai Tamil Arasu Kadchi.* Colombo: Ilankai Tamil Arasu Kadchi, 1956.

Vijayavardhana, D. C. *The Revolt in the Temple.* Colombo: Sinha Publications, 1953.

Vittachi, Tarzie. *Emergency '58.* London: Andre Deutsch, 1958.

Weerawardana, I. D. S. *Ceylon General Election, 1956.* Colombo: M. D. Gunasena & Co., Ltd., 1960.

————. *Government and Politics in Ceylon (1931-1946).* Colombo: Ceylon Economic Research Association, 1951.

What We Believe. Colombo: United National Party, 1963.

With the Masses into Action. Colombo: Lanka Sama Samaja Party, 1953.

Woolf, Leonard. *The Village in the Jungle.* London: Chatto & Windus, 1951.

Wriggins, W. Howard. *Ceylon: Dilemmas of a New Nation.* Princeton: Princeton University Press, 1960.

Wyndham, H. A. *Native Education.* London: Oxford University Press, 1933.

Articles and Papers

Ames, Michael. "Ideological and Social Change in Ceylon," *Human Organization* (special issue: "Contours of Culture Change in South Asia," ed. by William L. Rowe), XXII, 1 (Spring, 1963), 45-53.

Ariyaratnam, I. R. "Thirty Years of Communal Politics," *Forward*, July 2, 1965.

Balasuriya, P. B. "Bhāṣāvē Näṅgīma Jātiyē Näṅgīmayi [The Elevation of the Language is the Elevation of the Nation]," *Śrī Laṅkā Nidahas Pakṣayē Saṅvatsara Kalāpaya, 1964* [*Sri Lanka Freedom Party's Annual Number, 1964*]. Colombo: Sri Lanka Freedom Party, 1964, pp. 57-60.

Bandaranaike, S. W. R. D. "Message by the Prime Minister," *Śrī Laṅkā Nidahas Pakṣaya Sāṅvatsarika Kalāpaya, 1958* [*Sri Lanka Freedom Party Annual Number, 1958*]. Colombo: Sri Lanka Freedom Party, 1958, p. 15.

————. "Message by the Prime Minister and Leader of the Party," *Śrī Laṅkā Nidahas Pakṣaya Hatväni Sāṅvatsarika Kalāpaya, 1959* [*Sri Lanka Freedom Party Seventh Annual Number, 1959*]. Colombo: Sri Lanka Freedom Party, 1959, pp. 129-131.

Banks, Michael. "Caste in Jaffna," in E. R. Leach (ed.), *Aspects of Caste in South India, Ceylon and North-West Pakistan*. Cambridge Papers in Social Anthropology No. 2. London: Cambridge University Press, 1962, pp. 61-77.

Dassanayake, Ananda. "The Shame of Jaffna," *Ceylon Observer*, June 12, 1962.

De Souza, Doric. "Parliamentary Democracy in Ceylon," *Young Socialist* (Colombo), I, 3 (October-December, 1961), 125-139.

"Diary Leaves of the Late Ven. Anagarika Dharmapala," ed. by Sri D. Valisinha, serialized over a number of years in *Maha Bodhi* (Calcutta).

Evers, H. D. "Buddhism and British Colonial Policy in Ceylon, 1815-1875," *Asian Studies*, II, 3 (December, 1964), 323-333.

Fernando, Chitra. "Asian Xenophobia Against the West," *Annals of the American Academy of Political and Social Science*, CCCXVIII (July, 1958), 83-88.

Geertz, Clifford. "The Integrative Revolution: Primordial Sentiments and Civil Politics in the New States," in Clifford Geertz (ed.), *Old Societies and New States*. New York: Free Press of Glencoe, 1963, pp. 105-157.

Green, T. L. "Research in the Social Sciences in Ceylon University, Colombo," *International Social Science Bulletin*, III, 4 (Winter, 1951), 832-842.

Jayaraman, R. "Caste and Kinship in a Ceylon Tea Estate," *Economic Weekly* (Bombay), XVI, 8 (February 22, 1964), 393-397.

Jayasuriya, J. E. "Current Educational Trends and Controversies in Ceylon," *International Review of Education*, VIII, 3-4 (1963), 292-299.

Jayawardena, Kumari. "Anagarika Dharmapala and the Early Labour Movement in Ceylon," *Ceylon Daily News*, September 18, 1964.

————. "Birth Centenary of the Anagarika Dharmapala: His Impact on Politics Was Decisive and Far Reaching," *Ceylon Daily News*, September 16, 1964.

Jennings, Sir W. Ivor. "The Ceylon General Election of 1947," *University of Ceylon Review*, VI, 3 (July, 1948), 133-195.

————. "Communalism and the New Constitution." Article reprinted as a leaflet, from the *Hindu Organ*, December 10, 1945.

————. "The Languages of Ceylon," *University of Ceylon Review*, XI, 1 (January, 1953), 1-9.

————. "Politics in Ceylon," *Far Eastern Survey*, XXI, 17 (December 3, 1952), 177-180.

————. "Race, Religion and Economic Opportunity in the University of Ceylon," *University of Ceylon Review*, II, 1-2 (October, 1944), 1-13.

Kearney, Robert N. "Ceylon: The Contemporary Bureaucracy," in Ralph Braibanti and associates, *Asian Bureaucratic Systems Emergent from the British Imperial Tradition*. Durham, N. C.: Duke University Press, 1966, pp. 485-549.

————. "The Ceylon Communist Party: Competition for Marxist Supremacy," in Robert A. Scalapino (ed.), *The Communist Revolution in Asia*. Englewood Cliffs, N. J.: Prentice-Hall, Inc., 1965, pp. 373-398.

————. "The Marxists and Coalition Government in Ceylon," *Asian Survey*, V, 2 (February, 1965), 120-124.

————. "The New Political Crises of Ceylon," *Asian Survey*, II, 4 (June, 1962), 19-27.

————. "Sinhalese Nationalism and Social Conflict in Ceylon," *Pacific Affairs*, XXXVII, 2 (Summer, 1964), 125-136.

Lambert, Richard D. "Hindu Communal Groups in Indian Politics," in Richard L. Park and Irene Tinker (eds.), *Leadership and Political Institutions in India*. Princeton: Princeton University Press, 1959, pp. 211-224.

Mendis, G. C. "Adult Franchise and Educational Reform," *University of Ceylon Review*, II, 1-2 (October, 1944), 37-44.

Passé, H. A. "The English Language in Ceylon," *University of Ceylon Review*, I, 2 (November, 1943), 50-65.

Perera, L. S. "The Pali Chronicle of Ceylon," in C. H. Philips (ed.), *Historians of India, Pakistan, and Ceylon*. London: Oxford University Press, 1961, pp. 29-43.

Pieris, Ralph. "Bilingualism and Cultural Marginality," *British Journal of Sociology*, II, 4 (December, 1951), 328-339.

————. "New Elites in Ceylon," in *Transactions of the Fifth World Congress of Sociology*. Louvain, Belgium: International Sociological Association, 1964. Vol. III, pp. 295-302.

———. "Universities, Politics and Public Opinion in Ceylon," *Minerva*, II, 4 (Summer, 1964), 435-454.

Ryan, Bryce. "Status, Achievement and Education in Ceylon," *Journal of Asian Studies*, XX, 4 (August, 1961), 463-476.

———, L. D. Jayasena, and D. C. R. Wickremesinghe. "Secularization Processes in a Ceylon Village," *Eastern Anthropologist*, XI, 3-4 (March-August, 1958), 155-161.

Sarathchandra, E. R. "Some Problems Connected with Cultural Revival in Ceylon," *Bulletin of the Institute of Traditional Cultures, Madras*, 1962, Part I, pp. 1-11.

"Statement by Parliamentary Group of the Lanka Samasamaja Party (Ceylonese Section of the Fourth International) on the Language Question," *Fourth International*, No. 13 (Spring-Summer, 1961), p. 46.

Straus, Murray A. "Childhood Experience and Emotional Security in the Context of Sinhalese Social Organization," *Social Forces*, XXXIII, 2 (December, 1954), 152-160.

Tambiah, S. J. "Ceylon," in Richard D. Lambert and Bert F. Hoselitz (eds.), *The Role of Savings and Wealth in Southern Asia and the West*. Paris: UNESCO, 1963, pp. 44-125.

———. "Ethnic Representation in Ceylon's Higher Administrative Services, 1870-1946," *University of Ceylon Review*, XIII, 2-3 (April-July, 1955), 113-134.

Thani Nayagam, Xavier S. "Tamil Culture—Its Past, Its Present and Its Future with Special Reference to Ceylon," *Tamil Culture* (Madras), IV, 4 (October, 1955), 341-364.

Thillainathan, S. "Social Pattern in Jaffna," *Ceylon Observer*, June 25, 1962.

Tinker, Hugh. "People and Government in Southern Asia," in *Transactions of the Royal Historical Society*, Ser. 5, Vol. IX. London: Royal Historical Society, 1959, pp. 141-167.

Vanden Driesen, I. H. "Some Trends in the Economic History of Ceylon in the 'Modern' Period," *Ceylon Journal of Historical and Social Studies*, III, 1 (January-June, 1960), 1-17.

Wanasinghe, Sydney. "From Marxism to Communalism," *Young Socialist* (Colombo), III, 3 (June, 1965), 113-125.

Weerawardana, I. D. S. "The General Elections in Ceylon, 1952," *Ceylon Historical Journal*, II, 1-2 (July-October, 1952), 111-178.

———. "Minority Problems in Ceylon," *Pacific Affairs*, XXV, 3 (September, 1952), 278-287.

Weiner, Myron. "Political Integration and Political Development," *Annals of the American Academy of Political and Social Science*, CCCLVIII (March, 1965), 52-64.

Wilson, A. J. "Cultural and Language Rights in the Multi-National Society," *Tamil Culture* (Madras), VII, 1 (January, 1958), 22-32.

———. "Minority Safeguards in the Ceylon Constitution," *Ceylon Journal of Historical and Social Studies*, I, 1 (January, 1958), 73-95.

Newspapers

Ceylon Daily News (Colombo, daily).
Ceylon News (Colombo, weekly).
Ceylon Observer (Colombo, daily).
CMU Bulletin (Colombo, monthly).
Forward (Colombo, weekly).
Samasamājaya (Colombo, monthly).
Siṅhalē (Colombo, weekly).
Sunday Times of Ceylon (Colombo, weekly).
Times of Ceylon (Colombo, daily).
U.N.P. Journal (Colombo, weekly). Since 1962 published under the name *Siyarata.*

Other Sources

Kotelawala, Sir John. "Prime Minister's Speech, United National Party Eighth Annual Conference, 1956." (Mimeographed.) Colombo, 1956.
"Readership Survey, Ceylon, April-June 1964, Conducted for the Audit Bureau of Circulations Limited by the Market Research Department of Lever Brothers (Ceylon) Limited." (Mimeographed.) Colombo, September, 1964.
Suntharalingam, C. "Eelam: Our Deity." (Leaflet.) Jaffna: C. Suntharalingam, December 18, 1959.
United National Party. "Report of the Special Committee Appointed by the Working Committee to Inquire and Report within Three Months Generally on the Last General Election Campaign with Particular Reference to Defects if Any in the Said Campaign and Suggestions for Improvements of Similar Campaigns in the Future." (Mimeographed.) Colombo, [1960?].

INDEX

Abhayavardhana, Hector, 48n
All-Ceylon Buddhist Congress, 79
All-Ceylon Minority Tamils' Maha Sabha, 100
All-Ceylon Tamil Congress, *see* Tamil Congress
Ames, Michael, 42n
Ananda College, 43
Anti-śrī campaign, 86
Anuradhapura, 11, 44
Arasaratnam, S., 11n
Ariyaratnam, I. R., 132n
Arunachalam, Sir Ponnambalam, 26n, 28-29, 53
Aryan languages, 7-8, 16
Asoka, 9
Aziz, A., 105n

Balasuriya, P. B., 62n
Bandaranaike, S. W. R. D., 35-36, 61, 63-65, 68-69, 72, 76n, 77, 80-82, 85-88, 108, 109, 117, 121, 122, 130, 131n, 134
Bandaranaike, Sirimavo, 49, 60, 61-62, 109, 111, 114, 120-121, 123, 129, 134
Bandaranaike-Chelvanayakam Pact, 85-86, 107, 109, 117-119, 127, 131; text, 144-146
Banks, Michael, 99n
Bhasha Peramuna, 74, 77
Bhikkhus, 41-43, 79-80, 86, 88
Blavatsky, Helena Petrovna, 45
Bolshevik-Leninist party, 124n
Brahmin caste, 99
British colonial rule, 3, 12, 19, 24-25, 42n, 45-46, 52
Buddha Jayanti, 78-79
Buddharakkita, Mapitigama, 88
Buddhism, 7, 9, 41-42, 62, 137; *see also* Buddhist revival, Buddhists
Buddhist Committee of Inquiry, 79n
Buddhist revival, 41-47, 50, 71, 137
Buddhist Theosophical Society, 43, 45
Buddhists, 9, 41-43, 78-80, 133
Bureaucracy, *see* public service
Burghers, 7, 14, 15, 21, 26n, 30, 32
Burma, 42, 64

Caldecott, Sir Andrew, 40, 71
Cameron, C. H., 53, 55
Cartman, James, 49n, 99n
Caste, 4, 11, 23, 42, 99-101, 103
Ceylon Branch of the Royal Asiatic Society, 44
Ceylon Civil Service, 26, 53, 59n, 70
Ceylon Democratic Congress, 105
Ceylon Indian Congress, 104-105
Ceylon Moors, 7, 8, 14-16, 93n, 101-103, 134
Ceylon National Association, 26, 44
Ceylon National Congress, 26-30, 32, 33, 35, 36, 38-39, 44, 47-48
Ceylon Reform League, 26, 28
Ceylon Social Reform League, 44
Ceylon Tamils: size of community, 7; distribution, 8, 12; history, 10-12; educational opportunities of, 57, 66-67, 70; in the public service, 69-72; social mobility, 24
Ceylon Workers' Congress, 105-106, 115, 121, 129
Chamber of Commerce, 30
Chelvanayakam, S. J. V., 90-91, 93-94, 96-97, 102n, 106-110, 111, 115
Christian missionaries, 42, 49
Christian missionary schools, 24, 43, 45, 66
Christians, 14, 78, 122
Citizenship, 13, 90, 104-106, 108
Classes, *see* social classes
Coalition, Mahajana Eksath Peramuna, *see* Mahajana Eksath Peramuna coalition
Coalition, Sri Lanka Freedom party and Lanka Sama Samaja party, 127-129, 132-136
Colebrooke, W. M. G., 53, 55, 66n
Colombo, 4, 10, 14, 19, 28, 32, 53, 57, 86-87, 89
Colonial Office, 3, 34, 55
Colonial rule, 3, 16, 19-21, 45-49, 73, 79; *see also* Independence movement
Colonization schemes, 84, 95, 98, 118-119
Commission on Higher Education in the National Languages, 74